FAMOUS GHOSTS, PHANTOMS, AND
POLTERGEISTS FOR THE MILLIONS

"For the Millions" Series

FAMOUS GHOSTS, PHANTOMS, AND POLTERGEISTS FOR THE MILLIONS

by Andrew Tackaberry

FOR THE MILLIONS SERIES

SHERBOURNE PRESS, INC.   LOS ANGELES, CALIFORNIA

FOR JAMES B. SILVERMAN,
A PSYCHIC RESEARCHER PAR EXCELLENCE

Contents

CHAPTER ONE

Visions of the Night

What is a ghost? The answer to this question frequently depends on who is asked it. To most people a ghost is the stuff from which stories are written, the floating, white-clad, luminous form that is seen in deserted houses or in midnight graveyards moaning out messages of terror to the unsuspecting living. To others a ghost is the substance of dreams, appearing at the edge of sleep as the face of a loved one, long gone and almost forgotten, or as the nightmare symbol of all of his guilt and his fears. The child thinks of a ghost as bringing delightful shivers in stories, while the scientist considers the word "ghost" as being the collective term for all of the superstitious rubbish and useless myth of past ages.

A ghost? Why, a ghost is many things to many people, its nature depending upon the strength of their imaginations. But in this day and age it would be easier to say what a ghost is not. In the Age of Science, a ghost is not real. A ghost does not exist, and never did. A ghost, according to the average enlightened adult has no reality, but is merely the product of the credulous and fanciful mind.

Why then are there so many stories of ghosts and apparitions throughout the ages? Every country of the world has its ghostly stories and its customs and practices concerning the spirits of the dead and their position in the afterlife and in the living world. In myth and legend and in folklore, a ghost has a definite place and serves a distinct function, embodying in symbolic fashion the traditions and culture of a people. The modern intellectual can accept the idea of a ghost in this sense; he cannot, however, accept or admit that there is any reality to a ghost in the sense that it can be observed, studied, measured, or classified. The usual answer to those who say that they have seen or heard a ghost is "nonsense."

And yet there are countless reports of apparitions and ghostly visitations not given by the gullible or credulous, but by men and women of high intelligence and complete integrity. Other reports come from those who are complete skeptics and who could hardly credit their senses when encountering an apparition. These are the "real" ghost stories, as distinguished from fiction, that are the most interesting since they defy all reason and seem to have no basis in natural law to explain them.

The narratives that are presented here are meant to serve the reader as an introduction to some of the ghosts that have been encountered in the past and today. All types of people saw these ghosts: skeptics, frauds, scholars, the devoutly religious. The ghosts appearing are of all kinds, sad or vengeful, mischievous or solitary, rambunctious or silent. Some present themselves to the world of the living for a purpose, while others wander in and out of the world as aimlessly as a fleeting thought. Others appear in groups and bring the whole paraphernalia of

8

their earthly life back with them. Only in one case is a ghost found in a deserted house, and none linked to a graveyard. The supernatural is as varied as the natural world.

The term supernatural, of course, is seldom used now to refer to ghostly phenomena; a more exact word is paranormal, which means apart from or aside from the natural and the conventional. The study of paranormal or supernormal phenomena is parapsychology, which among other things embraces ghosts, apparitions, disembodied voices, telepathy, clairvoyance, poltergeists, and all of the phenomena which cannot be explained in terms of natural law or examined with the techniques of natural sciences. Another term for parapsychology is psychical research, which seems to be a more appropriate word to apply to the investigation of ghostly phenomena.

The psychical researcher approaches the study of ghosts and apparitions as a scientific observer seeking the explanation of the occurrences from the standpoint of ESP—extrasensory perception—which refers to the ability of some people to gain information and knowledge without the use of the usual five senses. There are several forms of ESP: telepathy, the perception of human thoughts without the use of the senses; clairvoyance, the perception of objects; telekinesis, the manipulation of objects without any discernible physical or sensory cause; precognition, the perception of future events; and others.

To the serious psychical researcher many accounts of ghosts and apparitions can be studied and explained in terms of ESP, and it is from this standpoint that he examines and investigates the phenomena. The difficulty of psychical research is in reproducing the phenomena in

9

the laboratory under proper experimental conditions to achieve any degree of repeatability. With the physical sciences this objective can be accomplished by the experimental researcher with a satisfactory measure of success. The mind, however, is considerably less easy to pin down; psychology itself is a relatively new form of study, while parapsychology to the traditional scientist is almost incomprehensible.

The problems of psychical research are enormous. The scientist views the field with scorn, the theologian with reservations, the layman with skepticism or with wonder. The reader must draw his own conclusions. But whatever the cause or explanation for apparitions and hauntings, the Book of Job still gives the best description of the feelings inspired by ghosts: "In thoughts from the visions of the night, when deep sleep falleth on men, Fear came upon me, and trembling, which made all my bones to shake. Then a spirit passed before my face; the hair of my flesh stood up; It stood still but I could not discern the form thereof; an image was before mine eyes."

CHAPTER TWO

A Plague of Phantoms

Although admitting a belief in ghosts today brands one as either infantile or disreputable, a simple explanation of the word can be given by anyone when asked. Why, of course, a ghost is a being that haunts houses and castles. A different person might suggest that a ghost is the spirit that returns to terrify his living descendants. And there, for the average person, the matter rests. The conversation is closed with a shrug of the shoulders and a rather scornful laugh which seems to say, "Of course, no sensible person could believe in such things as ghosts or haunted houses, not today."

Perhaps not, but to ignore the subject is to overlook a good portion of your culture and folklore, literature and poetry, mythology and legend, even—in a certain sense—religion. Regardless of the authenticity of ghost stories, they have a definite place in every society and serve a useful function, reflecting as they do the philosophic nature and cultural attitudes of every people.

Besides, if you ignore ghosts, you deprive yourself of the charm of their company.

Ghosts do more than float around deserted houses or moonlit graveyards, striking fear into the hearts of those to whom they appear. A brief glance at the table of contents in a few books devoted to the subject indicates that there is an almost infinite variety of ghosts, serving an equally large number of purposes. Some make their appearance to give a message to the living, some seek vengeance for wrongs done them in life, and others ask pitifully that they be given a proper burial. One type of ghost—the poltergeist—seems to exist solely to cause mischief and annoy reluctant hosts, though some poltergeists have been known to manifest a more sinister intention. Ghosts have been said to appear in dramatic reconstructions of the past, bringing with them clothing, furniture, and handicrafts long crumbled to dust, but furnishing again a sort of phantom stage setting.

The living may receive an apparition of a member of their family at the moment of death, or see a phantasm of the living who gives them warning of imminent physical danger. Injustices have been corrected by the visitations of ghosts, and other phantoms have helped to locate lost objects and papers, which have been known to provide comfort and financial aid to those left behind.

Specters have been seen that are reluctantly bound to the scenes of their earthly lives and appear to plead for release from the bondage of this world. Yet many a pet dog, cat, or horse has appeared in phantom form to their former masters, as if unwilling to be parted from their side.

Undoubtedly the largest number of ghosts have no purpose for their return to earth, none at least that can be determined by observers. It may be that the spirit has neither the power nor the ability to communicate the reasons for his appearances, or that the living observers are unable to understand. Both psychical researchers and professional mediums have attempted to enlarge the scope of communications with the spirits of the dead, claiming with some justification that the ordinary five senses are far from perfect as means of acquiring knowledge and achieving human awareness.

It would be difficult to draw up a strict listing of categories of ghosts and apparitions, although many writers attempt to do so. This chapter is meant merely to introduce the reader to a few of the types of ghosts he might meet.

Consider the story told by Pliny the Younger, of a house in Athens so notorious for being haunted that tenants could not be kept after hearing the sounds of dragging feet and clanking chains at night. The philosopher Athenodorus took the house in spite of its fearful reputation, probably because it was by then cheap. The ghost came to him during the first night spent there, clanking his shackles and beckoning fearfully at the philosopher to follow him. The skeletal and bearded figure led Athenodorus to a spot in the courtyard, which he indicated vigorously, then vanished. On the following morning Athenodorus persuaded the authorities to excavate the court, where they soon discovered the remains of the old man, still in his chains and manacles. The corpse was given a fitting burial then, and peace settled on the house.

In the summer of 1900 a phantom with a similar purpose was seen in Borley, England, by the four daughters of the church vicar. The ghost was the figure of a nun who frequently walked at the back of the rectory grounds and so often gazed wistfully in the window of Reverend Bull's study that the gentleman had the space bricked up. Nor was the ghostly sister a gliding wraith, but appeared in solid and opaque form; she was said to have appeared to more than a dozen persons on various occasions. Later investigations and experiments with a planchette indicated that the young nun had been murdered and secretly buried in the late seventeenth century and walked sorrowfully to request a proper reburial according to the rites of the Church. Some bones were later found by those investigating the phenomena surrounding Borley rectory and were given a Christian burial, even though there were doubts as to their belonging to the phantom nun.

Another English family in the 1880's witnessed an apparition who, because of the full black clothing she wore, was on several occasions taken to be a nun. This silent figure usually came to the Morton family in the house, though she was seen by some in the garden, but she evidently lacked the power of communicating her thoughts or giving a message. The figure walked through the upper halls and frequented the drawing room, where she would stand somberly peering out through the window. The ghostly figure, who was also solid and lifelike in appearance, was thought to be the unhappy widow of a former tenant, who in life caused her much distress by hiding some family jewels from her. If the ghost was searching for the long-hidden jewels, however, she failed in her purpose since she never appeared in the morning room where a cache for the jewels had been built under the floor. One of the more enterprising Morton girls asked the lady a number of times to tell them what she wanted, but with no success, so the ghost's purpose, if there was one, was never known.

Mischievous phantoms have been reported throughout history and in most countries of the world. The poltergeist, as this kind of spirit has come to be known, is possessed of the prankish, teasing nature of a child or adolescent, and seems to take great delight in upsetting a house. Stones and china are thrown about with abandon, furniture upset, bric-a-brac smashed, small but infuriating fires are frequently set. And should the recipients of these unwelcome attentions take to their beds to find peace, why, the poltergeist has been known to wave and rumple the sheets, even to throw them and the pillow to the floor.

The poltergeist has long been the favorite of the connoisseur of hauntings, perhaps because of the cheerful flamboyance of its manifestations. Such diverse writers as Sacheverell Sitwell, Father Thurston, and Hereward Carrington have written extensively of the noisy spirit. Indeed, Epworth Parsonage is famous to the ghost collector less as the birthplace of John Wesley than for the racket caused by the family's poltergeist, Old Jeffery. (See Chapter Four.)

A poltergeist favored the household of a Presbyterian clergyman, Reverend Phelps, at Stratford, Connecticut, in 1850. Here the spirit displayed greater virtuosity than the traditional noisemaker. It caused the fireplace tools to dance in the center of the floor, flung a potato at the head of the household, beat the floor repeatedly with a candlestick until it broke, threw the oldest son into the cistern, and, in a final burst of artistry, arranged the family clothing in the center of the kitchen to form a tableau of twelve female effigies at prayer. (See Chapter Five.)

The spirit that visited the Wesley family generally confined his activities to disturbing the peace of the rectory at night with loud knocks and raps on the walls and the

15

beds. The younger children of the family quickly became accustomed to what they called Old Jeffery, but the older daughters trembled at his nightly attentions. Mrs. Wesley implored the spirit to give her a few moments of peace so she might rest in the late afternoon, and the poltergeist complied with her request. Less patient was Mr. Wesley, who reportedly became extremely angry with the spirit for upsetting the household, shaking his fist toward its location and once threatening to shoot it.

The biting and scratching of the young children at Salem during colonial days has often been attributed to poltergeist activities, although the verdict of the authorities that sent so many to their deaths at the time was witchcraft. And in rural Tennessee in the nineteenth century, many of the afflictions suffered by the Bell family are considered to be characteristic of the poltergeist, yet few have shown so malicious a nature as to cause a broken engagement for a young girl and the death of her father.

By some unfathomable warp of time, the past has been restored to living observers, who saw and heard long dead spirits surrounded by their forgotten environment, complete with buildings, animals, and all types of useful worldly objects. Two English schoolteachers claimed to have walked into the memories of Marie Antoinette in 1901 at Versailles, as they strolled through the gardens surrounding the Petit Trianon laid out as they had been more than a hundred years before. The teachers said that they saw old gardening tools, a tiny bandstand, heard music from earlier operas, and saw and spoke to the courtiers of the executed queen. (See Chapter Eight.)

A more fearsome restoration of the past that happened in England was the fighting of the battle of Edge Hill,

16

two months after it had occurred on October 23, 1642. The original battle between the Royalist forces supporting Charles I and the opposing Parliamentary armies was violently and fiercely fought, though with no decisive results. Then shortly before Christmas of the same year some country people heard and saw the same battle being refought at the same place. Scarcely believing their senses, they reported their experiences to the local magistrates who, though considering the story improbable, accompanied the shepherds to the spot the next night, where they, too, witnessed the battle. The ghostly battle was fought again with the same ferocity, making the night ring with the crack of musketry, the screams of the wounded, and the thunder of the cannons. The King, on hearing of the affair, commanded a commission of six officers and gentlemen to the scene to squash the reports; these men also witnessed the battle in wonder, and testified under oath to the truth of the report, even being able to identify several of the soldiers who had died two months earlier.

One of the most mystifying phenomena to those experiencing it is seeing a phantasm of a living person or hearing an invisible voice. While such appearances frequently have occurred as portents of imminent death, there have been others reported that had less unhappy associations, and often foretold pleasant experiences. Once a woman novelist told of sitting in the drawing room of her London house on a warm summer's night when, at about nine o'clock, she looked up from her book and was pleasantly surprised to see a friend who had come to visit unannounced. The friend, Lord Campbell, walked toward her smiling through the hallway, holding a large bunch of sweet-smelling white lilacs as a gift, and his favorite dog padded at his side. The lady rose to greet her visitor and as she held out her hand, Lord Campbell and his dog both vanished. She was quite puzzled and more than a little worried, since she knew that such appearances of living phantasms often indicate death. An hour later, though, her fears were put to rest, when the same gentleman appeared in the same manner, holding the lilacs, with his dog frisking at his feet.

This lady also told of seeing a phantom of herself once while staying at a hotel in the south of France. She had been sleeping quite peacefully and toward dawn woke to see herself, or an apparition of herself, standing in the corner looking at her. The room was not in darkness but clearly lighted with the first dawn, and from the bed she watched, fully awake now, the ghostly lifelike figure of herself walk toward the bed and then, as she said, 'disappear into my body.'

Another case of self-apparition was told to Sir Oliver Lodge by a friend who was an archbishop. Here the gentleman saw a sort of mirror image of himself and his surroundings. He had returned to his home very tired one evening and sat down in an easy chair, only to fall deeply asleep. Some time later, less than an hour according to the clock, he awoke and looked up to see himself, though as a luminous wraith, gazing on him with interest and pleasure. At the side of the apparition he could see several books, which he knew were at his own side. The vision lasted for only a few seconds, according to F. S. Edsall who tells the story, and then disappeared, to return again briefly a few seconds later and again vanish as before.

The name of Sir Oliver Lodge appears in another curious account of the ghostly influence of the living. A woman was spending some days doing intensive reading and study in Lodge's book, *Man and Universe*, when she put the book down for a brief rest. When she returned to the book, which lay open on the table as she had left it, she noticed the pages turning. There were no open windows that would allow a breeze to flip the pages, so she looked back in wonder. She saw the pages being definitely turned as if by human hands, although invisible, as though the unseen reader was searching for a particular passage. This page turning happened on several occasions for several days. Finally the book was opened to a certain page and the leaves flattened out as though the unseen reader had found what he wanted. The lady took up the book and saw, in the margin, a cross scratched there as if done by a fingernail. On reading the marked passage, she discovered that it was the central thought and paragraph that she, too, had been searching for unconsciously.

Many times people have told of hearing the voices of their loved ones under odd circumstances when the persons are in distant places or parts of the world. These ghostly messages from the living often seem to come during a severe emotional crisis, or when the person is endangered. One woman was sailing back to England after a long trip to rejoin her husband. The ship had been buffeted for days by a severe and violent storm, and the lady finally fell to her bunk into an exhausted sleep, no longer caring about the outcome. Suddenly she was awakened by her husband's voice commanding her sharply to sit up. The command was repeated as clearly as if he was in the cabin with her. She did so unthinkingly just as a gigantic wave struck the ship and shattered the port-hole above her bunk, sending spears of glass deep into the pillow on which she had lain only moments before.

Can animals appear to their owners after death? So it would seem judging by the number of reports of such instances. One couple told that they were particularly upset by the death of their favorite bulldog, which they had had for years. But some days later they heard the dog back with them at their side, and recognized the sounds of his paws scratching the tiles and the asthmatic bulldog wheezing that characterized the breed. To their delight they even saw the animal many times lumbering across the floor and outside on the lawn, with the same expression of mock ferociousness and the wagging of the stubby tail that they knew so well. (See Chapter Nine.)

There are many reports of hearing phantasmal voices of the living telling of a family death. In general they usually happen when a couple of members of a family are widely separated and one of them hears the voice of the other informing him of the death of a child or parent. These cases are of great importance to the scientist, whether he is a psychologist, analyst, or psychical re-searcher, since they often seem to be based on the strong emotional ties between the separated parties and indicate the intense emotions that one is feeling. As an example, a merchant sailor told of being on the high seas, thousands of miles from home, when he heard the distressed voice of his wife crying out in anguish that one of their children was dead. The child had been in good health less than a week before, and the seaman was so startled that he took notice of the time and mentioned the incident to the mate. On reaching port he found a cable waiting which told him of the death of the child, on the same day and same time that he had heard his wife's cries.

Strong passions often provide the emotional foundations for seeing a ghost or an apparition. The sensitive and the psychically oriented recognize this in their investigations and feel that emotions linger in a room or a house. Such emotions can be felt by the living who are attuned to such matters. As they put it, they can take the atmosphere immediately of these disturbed places. This was demonstrated on a television program devoted to English haunted houses and starring the great actress, Margaret Rutherford, who conducted a tour of the reputedly haunted houses, accompanied by her husband and a professional psychic and medium. This gentleman stated flatly in several places that he knew not only that the room was haunted, but described the spirit that lingered there. The cameras even photographed what was claimed to be the manifestation, in the form of a wavering light, of a ghostly lady in a certain corridor of a mansion.

The wavering light in the film proves nothing, of course; films and photographs can be edited and doctored to present selectively whatever is desired. But the television presentation was done so skillfully, and with the professional artistry customarily associated with British television, that the average viewer needed no more proof than the shiver along his spine and his hair standing on end. Hopefully, some of the narratives of ghosts that follow may do the same for the reader.

CHAPTER THREE

The Phantom Widow

Legend, folklore, and written stories of the supernatural have accustomed people today to anticipate certain accepted conduct from a ghost, as well as conditioning them to an equally predictable form of emotional response. When confronted by an apparition of the dead, invariably clad in graveclothes and appearing usually at the stroke of midnight, a person is frozen in horrified awe which then grows to an overwhelming state of terror. Whether passed down through the generations by word of mouth or in written narratives, custom and tradition demand this almost ritual behavior. Both the phantom and his victim are expected to follow the time-worn patterns in performing their ghostly ballet. Modern supernatural fiction conforms to this formula, intentionally heightening the story's mood to produce in the main character and, hopefully, in the reader a feeling of uncontrollable horror.

It is interesting to observe how a person reacts in actual life, however, when confronted by the unknown and, in the case that follows, most certainly the uninvited. The files of any psychical researcher are full of such cases.

Among the most carefully studied and documented cases of haunting is that of a forthright red brick house at Bognor, Sussex, England, which for a seven-year period in the 1880's was frequently visited by a tall and thin woman dressed in black. This phantom, who was unknown to the occupants of the house, was later identified as the newly dead widow of the former owner. And the members of the family to whom she appeared responded with varying degrees of emotion, ranging from indifference to consuming scientific curiosity.

The visitations of the specter did not take place in a mouldering Gothic mansion, but in a sturdy, three-storied family residence, which had been built scarcely twenty years before. Nor did she present herself as a moaning and wavering trail of ectoplasmic mist at the stroke of twelve. Instead, her appearances—and they were attested to by at least seven competent observers—took place both at night and in broad daylight under the morning sun. The ghost appeared both within the house and outside, walking up the drive and in the orchard, and was most often found on the drawing room sofa by the bay window. Here, as would the lady of the house, she sat, complacently observing the everyday happenings in the outside world. As for the lady's tangibility, more than one of those fortunate enough to see her reported that she was so solid and opaque that on first appearances, at least, she was assumed to be a real and living person.

The reports of the hauntings at Bognor were investigated and recorded by Mr. Frederic W. H. Myers, one of the founders of the Society for Psychical Research. After interviewing the many witnesses of the apparition, studying and correlating their statements, Mr. Myers wrote an account under the title, "Record of a Haunted House," published in Volume VIII of the *Proceedings of the Society for Psychical Research.* He gave the pseudonym of Morton to the family involved to protect them from any resulting notoriety. It is his report and particularly the journal records of the haunting written by one of the percipients, Rose Morton, that lend an atmosphere of scientific credibility to the affair.

The house was built in 1860 in one of the more fashionable sections of the town and was bought before completion by Mr. S——— who took up residence with his wife and children, and lived there for some sixteen years until his death in 1876.

Mrs. S——— died shortly after the family moved into the house, leaving her husband, three or four children, depending upon the various reports, and a considerable amount of jewelry. Despondent over his wife's death, Mr. S——— sought his forgetfulness in the bottle, yet shortly afterward married for the second time, obeying the Victorian custom of finding a stepmother for his children as quickly as possible.

The second marriage of Mr. S——— was not a success. He was soon at odds with his new wife, quarreling bitterly, according to reports, as to the proper way of bringing up the children and, most important, to the disposition of his first wife's jewels. The second Mrs. S———, it seemed, considered the jewels to be hers by right of succession, but her husband felt that they should belong to his children, and took steps to remove them from the stepmother's hands. Calling in a carpenter, he ordered the man to make a hiding place for his dead wife's jewelry. The carpenter complied, taking up a portion of the floor in the morning room and building a secret compartment to hide the disputed jewels.

The quarrels between the couple continued and grew in intensity, "frequently resulting in violent scenes," as Mr. Myers wrote. Soon the second Mrs. S———, too, was drinking heavily, perhaps out of frustration from being denied the jewels she had so long sought, possibly to forget the dreariness of her married life. At length, having become fearful of her life and well being, Mrs. S——— left her husband and the house, moving to Bristol. The break was final. Mr. S——— died shortly afterward, on July 14, 1876, while his wife lived for two more years. Investigators of the case could find no evidence that Mrs. S——— ever returned to the unhappy house after her husband's death. She died alone, probably embittered and friendless, on September 23, 1878. Her Bristol death certificate gave as the cause of death: "Dipsomania, with intervening subgastritis."

The house was briefly occupied by Mr. L———, an elderly man in poor health, who died six months later. It stood vacant, then, until 1882 when it was rented to the Morton family. Captain Morton was acquainted with the present owner of the house, although he had not known the previous tenants, nor had he heard any stories of the house being haunted. He evidently found the house suitable for his large family, consisting of his invalid wife, four daughters, a son, and several servants. Another married daughter frequently visited with her husband, as did yet another son, who was away at school.

The Mortons moved into the house in the spring of 1882, and the appearances of the ghost began shortly afterward, in June. At first infrequent, the phantom's visits intensified during 1884, particularly during the months of July, August, and September. Afterward, the frequency of the appearances lessened over a period of years, as did their intensity. Gradually the apparition faded away, almost as if it was losing contact with its surroundings, until it finally disappeared in 1879 and was seen no more.

The ghost was heard by some twenty people, seven of whom also saw the figure and gave sworn statements describing their experiences. In these statements the various descriptions of the phantom's appearances agree in all relevant aspects. She appeared as a tall, thin woman clothed in black, and was unknown to any members of the household. The investigator interviewed the surviving members of Mr. S———'s family and, from their statements, concluded that the apparition was that of the second Mrs. S———. All descriptions of the ghost's appearance, dress, and behavior were verified by the survivors as agreeing with that of the dead stepmother.

It is perhaps significant that each witness to the apparition gave the same description, since the phantom, then, cannot be considered a subjective projection of the personality of the observer, such as a phantasm of the living or the so-called astral projection of someone intimately connected with the viewer. The Bognor apparition was unknown to all of the witnesses; the only connecting link was the house itself.

Nor did the ghost present herself in any frightening aspect, or indicate that she had a purpose or mission by appearing to the Mortons. None of the observers reported any feelings of terror when confronted by the specter, no seizures of fright, no inexplicable cold, clammy winds.

They could discern no reason for the ghostly visits and sensed no feelings of evil or malignancy directed toward them. In fact, in most reports given by the Mortons, the ghost appeared quite oblivious to their presence in what had once been her home.

Undoubtedly the most effective account of the apparition was given by nineteen-year-old Rose Morton. She was then a medical student who, although facing a totally incomprehensible situation, carefully and meticulously set down her observations of the ghostly visits in a daily journal as calmly as she might have kept records of a medical experiment. Of her attitude toward the phantom, she wrote: "In conclusion, as to the feelings aroused by the presence of the figure, it is very difficult to describe them; on the first few occasions, I think the feeling of awe at something unknown, mixed with a strong desire to know more about it, predominated. When I was able to analyse my feelings more closely, and the first novelty had gone off, I felt conscious of a feeling of loss, as if I had lost power to the figure."

Miss Morton wrote of the ghost in the form of a diary which she then sent as letters to Miss Catherine Campbell, a friend living in the North of England, and these letters give one of the most complete accounts of a haunting. The first appearance of the phantom in 1882 is best told in Rose Morton's words:

"I had gone to my room but was not yet in bed when I heard someone at the door and went to it, thinking it was my mother. On opening it I saw no one, but going a few steps along the passage I saw the figure of a tall lady, dressed in black, standing at the head of the stairs. After a few moments she descended the stairs and I fol-

27

lowed for a short distance, curious to see who it was. But I had only a small piece of candle and it suddenly went out. Seeing nothing more I went back to my room.

"The figure was of a tall lady wearing a dress of black, soft woolen material, to judge by the slight sound she made in moving. Her face was hidden in a handkerchief held in her right hand. This was all I observed then. Later, as I saw her repeatedly, I noticed more. Her left hand was nearly hidden by the sleeve and a fold in her dress. A portion of a widow's cuff was visible on both wrists, and gave the impression of a lady in widow's weeds. There was no cap on her head, but a general effect of blackness suggests a bonnet, with long veil or hood . . . Her footstep is very light, you can hardly hear it, except on the linoleum, and then only like a person walking softly with thin boots on."

On this initial visit by the ghost, Rose Morton first heard the phantom at her door, almost as if it was summoning her. She then saw the outline of the figure of the woman dressed in black some distance down the hallway. However, Miss Morton states that she noticed more details of the figure's clothing after repeated views of the apparition. It was almost as if the ghost was rather shy and timid in its first appearance, but was reassured by the girl's attitude of simple curiosity, not fear, and thus presented itself more clearly and confidently on the subsequent visits.

During the next two years, the ghost came to Rose at least a half dozen times, remaining visible for longer periods, and was also seen by three others in the house. The married daughter, Mrs. K———, came across the ghost one day downstairs and took the figure for a Sister of Mercy, who had called earlier. On another occasion, the youngest Morton son was playing with a companion on the terrace outside the drawing room when they looked up and saw the figure standing at the window, weeping bitterly. And again, a housemaid who saw the ghost reported the figure as an intruder; a search of the house disclosed nobody, however.

With her curiosity aroused by the ghost's first appearance, Rose Morton made efforts to pursue the figure on its later visits. She followed the ghost down the stairs on the later occasions and into the drawing room. There the figure would pause and stand looking out of the bay window, and then move on to the garden door and disappear. While the figure seemed to summon the girl by the sounds and footsteps past her bedroom door, it took no notice of her following into the drawing room. In January of 1884, Miss Morton attempted to communicate with the phantom for the first time and, from her account, the figure apparently seemed to have noticed her:

"I opened the drawing room door softly and went in, standing just by it. She entered, passed me, and walked to the sofa, where she stood still. So I went up to her and asked if I could help her. She moved and I thought she was going to speak but only gave a slight gasp and moved to the door. Just by the door I spoke to her again, but she seemed as if she were quite unable to speak. She walked into the hall and then disappeared by the side door as before."

Again, it is clear that the ghost made no attempts to frighten the girl, nor did she indicate that there was any mission connected with her appearances. She simply announced her coming by the sounds of her footsteps and the movements of her heavy skirts. She then made herself visible, as Miss Morton wrote, " . . . outlines being very distinct, and the whole appearance solid," so much so that other observers mistook her for a living person.

By now Rose Morton had seen the figure appear and disappear so often that she must have realized that she was facing the supernatural. Yet, undaunted, she continued in her efforts to make contact and communicate with the woman in widow's weeds. She began experiments to test the reality of the figure:

"The following May and June I tried experiments, fastening strings with marine glue across the stairs at different heights. I saw her pass through them at least twice. Also, I tried to touch her, but she always eluded me. Not that there was nothing to touch but she always seemed beyond me, and if I followed her into a corner, she simply disappeared. During the two years, 1882–1884, the only noises I heard were of slight pushes against my bedroom door accompanied by footsteps, and if I looked out I invariably saw the figure."

During the summer of 1884 the hauntings reached their peak, and the ghost was heard and seen by the greatest number of observers, in the most varied situations and surroundings. One evening late in July the figure appeared to Rose Morton much to the girl's amazement, since she came to the drawing room where Rose sat with her father and sisters. The phantom walked through the room and stood behind the sofa on which Rose sat, but was visible only to her; neither Captain Morton nor his other daughters saw the figure. Captain Morton had not at this time been told of the apparition by his family. "She stood behind the couch for about half an hour, and then as usual walked to the door. I went after her, on the excuse of getting a book, and saw her pass along the hall, until she came to the garden door, where she disappeared. I spoke to her as she passed the foot of the stairs, but she did not answer, although as before she stopped and seemed as though about to speak."

The phantom widow appeared again at the beginning of August and was again spoken to, but was either unwilling or unable to speak. On the following night the same spectral feet were heard walking in the upstairs passage. "On the night of August 2nd the footsteps were heard by my three sisters and by the cook, all of whom slept on the top landing—also by my married sister, Mrs. K———, who was sleeping on the floor below. They all said the next morning that they heard them very plainly pass and repass their door . . . These footsteps are very characteristic, and are not at all like those of any of the people in the house; they are soft and rather slow, though decided and even. My sisters would not go out on the landing after hearing them pass, nor would the servants, but each time when I have gone out after hearing them, I have seen the figure there."

Upon questioning, the cook stated that she had heard the footsteps before and had on two occasions seen the figure, once at night and once during the day. Her description of the figure and how it was dressed agreed with what Rose had so often seen. Rose then told her father of the incidents, writing, ". . . he was astonished because he had heard and seen nothing. Nor had my mother, but she was slightly deaf and an invalid."

The specter in black appeared often during August to members of the Morton household. She was seen by Mrs.

K———, the eldest Morton daughter, in full daylight standing on the garden terrace and looking through the drawing room window. On the same day the figure appeared twice in the drawing room, once to Rose Morton, the second time to a younger sister. On the next day the ghost appeared four times; she was seen walking through the orchard by Mrs. K———, later walking up the carriage drive by Rose. Then, in the evening, the figure was seen by Edith Morton in the back drawing room, standing and watching by the piano while the younger daughter was playing. An hour or so later she came to Rose in the same room. Three days later the ghost was seen walking in a lower hallway by a parlormaid, who claimed to have suffered a slight facial paralysis as a result of the shock. The attending physician, however, ascribed the woman's muscle condition to sleeping in a draft.

The years 1884–1886 marked the period during which the ghost manifested itself with the greatest frequency and intensity in the Morton house. In Miss Morton's words, "The footsteps continued, and were heard . . . in all by about 20 people . . . Other sounds were also heard in addition, which seemed gradually to increase in intensity. They consisted of walking up and down on the second-floor landing, of bumps against the doors of the bedrooms, and of the handles of the doors turning . . . A second set of footsteps was also heard, heavy and irregular, constantly recurring, lasting a great part of the night, often three or four times a week. On the first floor the same sounds are heard, especially in the front right-hand room, formerly used by Mr. and Mrs. S———. Louder sounds were also heard in the summer of 1885, heavy thuds and bumpings, especially on the upper landing."

32

Frederick Myers interviewed the members of the Morton family in 1896 after being told of the events occuring in the house. Of the Mortons he wrote, "It must be added that Captain M——— and the members of his family in general, while feeling little scientific interest in the apparition, were unusually free from superstitious fears." Yet Rose Morton indicates that her family shared her curiosity about the apparition, since she wrote that the family joined her on numerous occasions in making "special arrangements to watch for it." She herself, at Mr. Myers suggestion, attempted to photograph the ghost's appearances, and seemed quite disappointed when bad lighting conditions resulted in the experiment's failure.

Miss Morton during the hauntings did her utmost in attempting to apprehend and communicate with the spirit. "I constantly spoke to the figure, asking it to make signs if it was unable to speak, but got no response. On cornering it, as I did once or twice, the figure vanished. I tried suddenly to pounce on it, but could never touch it . . . She always intercepted the light but I could not ascertain if she ever cast a shadow."

After 1886 the figure was rarely seen and on those few occasions appeared in a less substantial form. The footsteps were still heard but those, too, were becoming softer. Several times the sounds of walking were heard by Mrs. Morton, her daughters, and the housemaids. Upon investigating the women saw no apparition, but did see lights flickering in the lower hallway, which they said were similar to candle flames. Then they heard the ghost walking up and down the staircase repeatedly, and felt a cold wind pass over them. Still, they saw nothing, however,

33

nor did their own candles go out when the wind passed over them.

The ghost seemed to be losing its power to manifest herself in her earthly surroundings and grew fainter and less distinct, both in appearance and by sound, in 1887 and 1888. During the entire seven-year period of the hauntings, the phantom widow gave no indication of her reasons for returning to the house in which she had been so unhappy. Strangely enough, she never appeared in the back room in which the disputed jewels were hidden, the same room in which her husband, Mr. S——, was found dead. Nor did she try to communicate with the Mortons. She simply appeared, even during the strongest period of her visitations, somewhat as a rather wistful on-looker of the happy domestic life of the Morton family. And then she faded away, and after 1889 was seen no more.

CHAPTER FOUR

Life with the Wesleys

It is so easy for a young college student, for the first time away from home, to be lax in writing his parents for news of his friends and family. Often before he realizes it, he lets weeks slip by without writing. Then, feeling a bit homesick and perhaps a little guilty, he sends a short note home and waits expectantly for a letter by return mail, full of the homely, placid details about his family and their common, everyday affairs.

Imagine his surprise, however, if he receives a letter as startling as the following (abridged for brevity):

January, 12, 1716

Dear Sam,

This evening we were agreeably surprised with your pacquet, which brought the welcome news of your being alive, after we had been in the greatest panic imaginable, almost a month, thinking either you was dead, or one of your brothers by some misfortune been killed.

The reason of our fears is as follows. On the first of December our maid heard, at the door of the dining-room, several dismal groans, like a person in extremes, at the point of death. We gave little heed to her relation, and endeavoured to laugh her out of her fears. Some nights (two or three) after, several of the family heard a strange knocking in divers places, usually three or four knocks at a time, and then stayed a little. This continued every night for a fortnight; sometimes it was in the garret, but most commonly in the nursery, or green chamber . . .

Thus it continued till the 26th of December, when it loudly knocked (as your father used to do at the gate) in the nursery and departed. We have various conjectures what this may mean. For my own part, I fear nothing now you are safe at London hitherto, and I hope God will still preserve you. Though sometimes I am inclined to think my brother is dead. Let me know your thoughts on it.

S.W.

Susannah Wesley, the mother of Methodism's founder, wrote this letter to her eldest son, Samuel, who was then at school at Westminster. In it Mrs. Wesley describes at length and with some degree of agitation, the psychical phenomena that plagued the rectory at Epworth for a two-month period, where she lived with her husband, the Rev. Mr. Samuel Wesley, and those of her nineteen children still at home. While authorities disagree as to the exact dates of the strange events and the letters—some say November and December, others December and January, while others put the year as 1719 and dispute the reality of the phenomena—all admit that the affair constitutes one of history's most fascinating studies of the poltergeist.

Robert Southey's *Life of John Wesley* gives a two-page account of the haunting of Epworth Rectory, but a greater sense of immediacy is gained by learning of the affair from the Wesley family letters—young Samuel's questioning notes and his family's answers—written shortly afterward, as well as from Mr. Wesley's journal, and statements taken from the family some years later by the younger son, John.

The authenticity of the phenomena themselves has been challenged by many writers and students, following the lead of Frank Podmore, who felt the so-called supernormal affair to be the result of pranks of one of the children. Again, some authorities claim that the Wesley household was actually infested by a poltergeist. Arguments can be given to support either point of view, of course. But if one cannot prove the existence of an actual poltergeist from examining the letters and statements of the family, he can, at least, discover the human qualities of the Wesleys—humor, anxiety, irritability, infectious high spirits, and courage—qualities which have too long been frozen into the pietistic attitudes of a Victorian steel engraving showing a family at prayer.

The Rev. Mr. Wesley received a royal bounty of a home at Epworth in Lincolnshire and a cash stipend acknowledging his epic *Life of Christ*. This crown living began in 1696, after Wesley struggled for years with the unremunerative living at South Ormsby. The living at Epworth, larger and richer than South Ormsby, must have appeared as a blessing to the struggling clergyman, who always found it difficult to make ends meet and properly house his family of twenty. Susannah Wesley had by the age of forty borne nineteen children, or "pledges of affection," of whom John and Charles, names revered in the history of Methodism, were the fifteenth and eighteenth.

Despite the royal favor which gave him the living, Mr. Wesley did not find life easy at Epworth. The parishioners were decidedly hostile and suspicious; natives of Lincolnshire had long been known for their activities in witchcraft and the darker arts and resented any newcomer. The villagers openly refused to tithe, as was then the custom, and expressed their hostility toward the new vicar in a distinctly unpleasant manner. The barn fell down, or was demolished, followed by the burning of the rectory. When a second rectory was built it, too, was destroyed by fire. At length, the third rectory was constructed of brick and this managed to last and form the scene of the strange events twenty years later. All of this house building was expensive, naturally, and Mr. Wesley found it increasingly difficult to meet his obligations until finally he was forced into debtors' prison for several months to satisfy his creditors.

Apart from these occasional outbursts of belligerence by the parishioners, life at the Epworth rectory was relatively placid, though frugal and devout. The Wesleys were a devoted and God-fearing couple, whose affection was marred only by a difference of opinion in politics. Mr. Wesley's Whig leanings found it hard to countenance his wife's Jacobite beliefs, particularly her refusal to join in the family prayers for William of Orange and his royal successors. John Wesley later wrote of the resulting quarrel between his parents: "He vowed he would never cohabit with her till she did. He then took his horse and rode away, nor did she hear anything of him for a twelve-month. He then came back and lived with her as before. But I fear his vow was not forgotten before God." This separation between the couple took place in 1701–02. The disagreement was patched up, of course, and life continued as before in the house for some fifteen years.

And then the noises began.

As Susannah Wesley wrote to her son, the first intimation of the affliction was the strange moaning at the door heard by a maidservant, who thought it might have been made by an extremely sick visitor. No person was found, however, and her employers ignored her story. Within a day or two, both the Wesley children and the servants were hearing the mysterious sounds, which they described as knocking and rapping all over the house, on every floor and in most rooms, especially in the nursery. In addition to the knocking, the sounds included those of a man's footsteps going up and down on the stairs all night and what was described as "vast rumblings" below stairs and in the attic. After several days and nights of these inexplicable occurrences the children were distinctly uneasy and frightened. They knew that their father should be told, but probably were as nervous about telling him as they were in undergoing the plague of strange sounds. The father of nineteen children undoubtedly held a firm grip on the disciplining of his children, and Mr. Wesley was not a man to accept frivolous nonsense, as the letters indicate.

At length Mrs. Wesley felt that her husband must be told of the affair, since she was unable to discover its cause. According to John Wesley in the *Arminian Maga-*

zine in 1784, his father's response was typical of all fathers everywhere: "But he was extremely angry, and said, 'Suky, I am ashamed of you; these boys and girls frighten one another, but you are a woman of sense and should know better. Let me hear of it no more!' "

In spite of Mr. Wesley's refusal to believe, the strange rappings continued. Mrs. Wesley thought the cause might be rats and weasels scampering about the walls and in the attic, and, having been successful with the procedure once before, she again had horns blown loudly throughout the house to drive away the pests. The result was that the rappings grew louder and more persistent.

The older girls continued their efforts to make their father believe in the poltergeist but, as Emily wrote Samuel, "He smiled and gave no answer, but was more careful than usual, from that time, to see us in bed, imagining it to be some of us young women, that sat up late and made a noise. His incredulity, and especially his imputing it to us, or our lovers, made me, I own, desirous of its continuance till he was convinced."

At last it became Mr. Wesley's turn to hear Old Jeffery, as Emily named the poltergeist. When in bed the next night Mr. Wesley heard nine loud and distinct knocks on the wall by his bedside, the rappings being made in groups of three. Still wondering if the noises were being made either by the children or by somebody outside the house, he rose and searched the house and grounds to discover the cause, but saw nothing. "Afterwards he heard it as the rest," Mrs. Wesley wrote. Still thinking that there must be a natural explanation for these unwanted noises, Mr. Wesley bought a "stout mastiff," hoping that the watchdog would discover the culprits and frighten them away. But on the next night, when six similar rappings were heard, the dog began to bark in a fury and then suddenly fell silent and began to grovel in terror, as it continued to act throughout the affliction.

About two nights later the Wesleys were awakened by what Mrs. Wesley in her first letter to Samuel described as: ". . . such a noise in the room over our heads as if several people were walking, then run up and down stairs and was so outrageous that we thought the children would be frightened, so your father and I rose and went down in the dark to light a candle. Just as we came to the bottom of the broad stairs, having hold of each other, on my side there seemed as if somebody had emptied a bag of money at my feet; and on his, as if the bottles under the stairs (which were many) had been dashed in a thousand pieces." The couple found a candle in the kitchen, which they lighted, and went in search of the reason for the disturbance. They found nothing, and in the nursery the children were sound asleep, yet, according to Mr. Wesley, "We still heard it rattle and thunder in every room, locked as well as open, above and behind us."

And still no plausible explanations could be discovered to account for the disturbances. It was not rats or weasels, as the horn-blowing episode proved, nor could it be proved that the children or their friends had been playing jokes on their parents. When his mother first wrote of the affair, young Samuel also expected that natural reasons could be found; in one letter he asked his mother if a new maid or manservant could be playing tricks. He then asks if anyone was walking in the garret during the disturbances, or were the sounds heard by the entire family when they were together in one room at one time. He thinks that his mother should consider the possibility of cats, rats, or dogs being the "sprights," but doesn't overlook the possibility of some of his brothers and sisters playing pranks: "Did it seem to be at all in the same place, at the same time? . . . Was the whole family asleep when my father and you went downstairs?" He concludes the letter with the postscript, "I expect a particular account from every one."

Susannah Wesley's letter to her son admits that she had considered all the points he had mentioned earlier. The servants, she said, were the most frightened of all during the racket, beside which they were with the family in the same room. As to his other suggestions, "All in the family heard it together, in the same room, at the same time, particularly at family prayers. It always seemed to all present in the same place at the same time, though often before any could say it was here, it would remove to another place." When the knocking came and the parents went to search for the cause, the family was asleep, ". . . nor did they wake in the nursery when we held the candle close by them, only we observed that Hetty trembled exceedingly in her sleep, as she always did before the noise awakened her. It commonly was nearer her than the rest, which she took notice of, and was much frightened, because she thought it had a particular spite at her . . ." Mrs. Wesley then informs Samuel that his father will write soon and elaborate.

Samuel had to write his father twice before Mr. Wesley responded, and the vicar's short note could hardly be considered an elaboration, saying only, "As for the noises, etc., in our family, I thank God we are now all quiet. There were some surprising circumstances in that affair.

Your mother has not written you a third part of it. When I see you here, you shall see the whole account which I wrote down . . ."

Some of his sisters, though, did write Sam; the letters are undated and were probably written after the noises stopped. Perhaps they might have been written during the two-month period of infestation, although this is unlikely considering the commotion in the house. The letter sent by his sister Susannah is interesting; while saying that their father will write a larger account of the matter, she describes briefly what they have undergone and in most respects her statements agree with that of her mother. However, while telling that she has heard the sound of a man walking by her bedside as if he were wearing a long nightgown, she also implies that something has been seen: "To conclude this, it now makes its personal appearance; but of this more hereafter. Do not say one word of this to our folks, nor give the least hint."

By this time the family, and most particularly the girls, were familiar with the characteristic noises that signalled the beginning of the night's racketing. Usually starting about ten o'clock at night the sound was variously described by those who heard it as "the strong winding up of a jack," or "the turning of a windmill when the wind changes."

On one especially riotous night this signal was followed by knockings throughout the kitchen in all corners of the room, and then tapping in the nursery again, banging on the floor at the foot of the bed, the walls by its side, and then on the headboards of the bed itself. Apparently out of temper by now, Mr. Wesley chased the turmoil around the kitchen, beating on the joists and rafters of the room, but to no effect; his own raps were consistently answered by Old Jeffery. Mr. Wesley then went up to the nursery, where the sounds were again happening, accompanied by a neighboring vicar, Mr. Hoole, who was visiting for the night. Mr. Hoole described that evening to John Wesley much later, saying, "We then heard a knocking over our heads, and Mr. Wesley, catching up a candle, said, 'Come, sir, you shall now hear for yourself.' We went up-stairs, he with much hope, and I (to say the truth) with much fear . . . And there it continued to knock, though we came in, particularly at the head of the bed (which was of wood) in which Miss Hetty and two of her younger sisters lay. Mr. Wesley, observing that they were much affected, though asleep, sweating and trembling exceedingly, was very angry, and, pulling out a pistol, was going to fire at the place from whence the sound came. But I catched (sic) him by the arm and said, 'Sir, you are convinced this is something preternatural. If so, you can-not hurt it, but you give it power to hurt you.' He then went close to the place and said, sternly, 'Thou deaf and dumb devil, why dost thou frighten these children that cannot answer for themselves? Come to me to my study that am a man! Instantly it knocked his knock (the par-ticular knock which he always used at the gate) as if it would shiver the board in pieces, and we heard nothing more that night."

Until this time, Mr. Wesley's study was the one room in the rectory not yet afflicted. But as if accepting his chal-lenge the "deaf and dumb" spirit soon began plaguing the study, not only with the customary racketing, but with physical retaliation also. On one occasion Mr. Wesley felt himself pushed with tremendous force hard against his desk, and another time the spirit used overwhelming strength to shove him into the door. And on a third visit Old Jeffery, as if claiming victory over the beleaguered clergyman, threw him violently into the door jamb as Mr. Wesley was escaping the room.

Other physical manifestations demonstrated to the Wesleys included raising the door latch in the kitchen in the presence of members of the family. Young Emilia Wesley used all the force she could summon to force the latch down into place, but the spirit persisted, all the while pushing the door forcefully against the girl. The same door latch was seen to lift itself, or be lifted, many times—and these were not the light modern latches known today, but heavy and sturdy iron and beam contraptions. The spirit also managed to interrupt a game of cards the girls were playing in the nursery by lifting the bed on which Nancy Wesley sat, so sharply that the girl refused to continue the game or sit on the bed.

The younger children seemed to accept the spirit toward the end of the time of the manifestations, and took a certain delight in annoying Old Jeffery. Emily wrote, "It would answer to my mother if she stamped on the floor and bid it. It would knock when I was putting the children to bed, just under me where I sat. One time little Kezy, pretending to scare Patty as I was undressing them, stamped with her foot on the floor, and immediately it answered with three knocks, just in the same place. It was more loud and fierce if anyone said it was rats or anything natural."

Sister Susannah also told her brother of the spirit's apparent physical powers: "One thing I believe you do not know—that is, last Sunday, to my father's no small amazement, his trencher danced upon the table a pretty while, without anybody's stirring the table. When lo! an adventurous wretch took it up, and spoiled the sport, for it remained still ever after. How glad should I be to talk with you about it. Send me some news, for we are secluded from the sight, or hearing, of any versal thing except Jeffery."

Sam had asked if any of the family had seen anything during the affair, as well as hearing noises, since he felt the evidence of two senses to be better than one. Emilia, in her long reply, told of Hetty being followed down the stairs by a man wearing a long white robe, but doesn't make clear whether Hetty actually saw an apparition, or simply heard the swishing sounds the others had heard. She says, however, that she herself saw something "that was discernible," and that the manservant, Robert Brown, twice saw an unaccountable creature. The first time, when in the dining room, he saw a strange badger-like animal run out from under the table. Later in the kitchen one night he again saw another peculiar creature. "After nine, Robert Brown, sitting alone by the fire in the back kitchen, saw something come out of the copper-hole, like a rabbit but less, and turn around five times very swiftly. Its ears lay flat upon its neck, and its little scut stood straight up."

The same Robert Brown heard the spirit another time, according to Mr. Wesley: "My man, who lay in the garret, heard someone come slaring through the garret to his chamber, rattling by his side as if against his shoes, though he had none there; at other times walking up and down stairs, when all the house were in bed, and gobbling like a turkey-cock."

Mr. Wesley reports in his journal that he had attempted

to communicate with what he now considered a spirit, commanding once that if the thing was the spirit of his son, Samuel, it should answer by knocking three times. To his joy, there was no further sound, and the family took this to mean that Samuel was still among the living. Again, after following the noises both day and night to determine its nature, "when I heard a noise, spoke to it to tell me what it was, but never heard any articulate voice, and only once or twice two or three feeble squeaks, a little louder than the chirping of a bird, but not like the noise of rats, which I have often heard."

And so the noisy, troublesome disturbances continued to plague the Wesley family in the Epworth rectory until the end of January, when it ceased—or the spirit, old Jeffery, departed—and was heard no more.

What caused the disturbances? Why did they happen? For two hundred fifty years these questions have been asked, and many opinions given in answer, ranging from that which claims a hoax foisted on the parents by one or more of the Wesley children, to the school of thought which sees in the affair an authentic and classic example of an infestation by a poltergeist.

It may safely be assumed that the disturbances were not caused by neighboring villagers bent on continued annoyance and vandalism. The Wesleys searched for such troublemakers, accompanied by a mastiff, and found nothing. And a watchdog worthy of his name would not cower in fright when confronted by intruders on a dark night.

Could the Wesley children have joined together in playing pranks on their parents? Some of the disturbances might be accounted for in this manner, but not all. The animals seen by the manservant, Robert Brown, could have easily been a badger and a rabbit brought into the house secretly by the children and hidden in the dining room and kitchen. But the banging and knocking about the house late at night could not have been caused by the children, who were found asleep at these times. They could have been feigning sleep, of course; joining together to rap and knock in various parts of the house, then racing back to the nursery to jump in bed just before their parents came in. While this is possible, it is improbable that a group of young children could sustain its interest in such a game for a period of two months.

Volume XVII of the *Proceedings of the Society for Psychical Research,* published in 1903, presents the views of two members concerning the possibility of the affair being a prank. Mr. Frank Podmore states this viewpoint clearly, an opinion that has been agreed with by most students of the phenomena. Mr. Andrew Lang, however, discounts Podmore's views in a series of letters, answering Podmore's objections.

In Podmore's opinion the prankster responsible for the Epworth disturbances was Hetty Wesley, claiming that the so-called poltergeist was always at its noisiest in Hetty's vicinity. By citing the reports that Hetty was found by her parents trembling and sweating in her sleep, Podmore implies that she was feigning sleep, after rapping on the walls about the house. Hetty did not write her brother Samuel at the time of the disturbances, nor did she give an account of the affair to John Wesley in 1726, when the other members of the family gave theirs. In fact, it is the letters and accounts written by the various Wesleys that seems to form the basis for Podmore's belief; he feels that the accounts do not at all agree in details, and that many of the statements written in 1716 were later embellished by the Wesleys in 1726.

Andrew Lang replies to Podmore's objections by pointing out that the other children were found undergoing troubled sleep as well as Hetty Wesley on all occasions. Nor did the disturbances happen only near Hetty; she was not always present when the door latches were lifted or the sounds were made of bottles breaking and money being scattered. While Hetty, it was said, felt that the spirit showed the greatest spite toward her, what of the spite shown to Mr. Wesley in his study? The girl was not present when Mr. Wesley felt himself being thrown against the furniture and into the door, Lang says.

Nor can Hetty be considered the instigator of pranks simply by the fact that she did not write her brother of the affair in 1716, or give an account in 1726. Neither Molly nor Nancy Wesley wrote Samuel during the disturbances, Lang states, and as for her not giving an account to brother John ten years later, this is easily explained by the fact that she had married against her father's wishes and was, at the time, living some distance from Epworth in disgrace.

Lang concludes his answer by stating that, in his opinion, the trickster was the new maidservant, basing this view simply on the fact that the disturbances began with her arrival in the household and that she was the last recorded percipient of the phenomena. While this, on the surface, seems a rather weak argument without further development, the editors of the *Proceedings* finally called a halt to this exchange of views, and no further amplification was given.

Both Podmore and Lang agree that the Epworth phenomena were the result of tricks, while disagreeing on the person responsible. But could the disturbances actually have been caused by a poltergeist instead of children's tricks? A poltergeist is usually considered a spontaneous psychical manifestation centered around the person of a child at the onset of puberty, and characterized by strange and unaccounted rappings and noises and, especially, by the throwing of objects. While at Epworth there were no reports of things actually being thrown, but only noises, the rapping and knocking in the house could, if the accounts were accurate, be considered as caused by a poltergeist. Hetty Wesley at about nineteen could not be thought of as a child, of course.

Sacheverell Sitwell in his book *Poltergeists* makes a strong case for an actual poltergeist at the bottom of the Epworth case. Hetty's troubled sleep, he feels, might well be thought of as a mediumistic trance in which strong psychical energies focus on her person and function through her. In this view a medium is simply the agent, unconsciously, for the transmission of unknown energies, perhaps of the subconscious, possibly of the spirit world. If one agrees with this, Hetty Wesley could be thought of as functioning unconsciously as the medium of the so-called poltergeist's energies, or even as the poltergeist itself.

There are points in favor of all of these views, and many other explanations can be offered for the Epworth phenomena. Certainly Mr. Wesley was correct when he wrote that his wife had not told their son a third of the surprising circumstances. And of the many possible interpretations given the matter, young Sam Wesley seems to have had the last word: "Wit, I fancy, might find many, but wisdom none."

50

CHAPTER FIVE

Poltergeists and Rowdy Spirits

The night is quiet, the lights are on in the house. Upstairs the children sleep innocently in their beds, undisturbed and peaceful. Suddenly rapping occurs, light and unobtrusive. The taps increase, louder and more insistent. Then from another room there comes a resounding crash!

Investigation proves that somebody forgot to put a skillet back in the pantry. Did the pan slip accidentally to the floor? But it was found in the center of the kitchen, a full ten feet from the door to the pantry.

Many a person has had just such an experience. In most cases the explanation is obvious. The skillet had not been stored away in its usual place, but had been forgotten and left precariously sitting on the edge of the sink. A damp porcelain surface, a slight shifting of the house—and even the newest modern homes will sway and give to the wind—usually explains the racket, along with the normal absent-mindedness common to most adults. The incident is laughed at and forgotten, since it can easily happen in any household.

But what caused the rapping?

Strange tapping noises can always be explained by the rational mind. The average healthy adult can easily shrug aside events of an apparent occult nature; only the emotionally disturbed could be frightened by the unexpected manifestations which often happen in everyday life, and only the advanced neurotic would generally become obsessed.

But in isolated instances the nightly rapping may repeat itself, not only at night but during the day. The disturbances may grow in power and in force, the dropping of common objects might assume the proportions of hurling the articles from room to room, resulting in malicious destruction. There are cases on record of small and annoying fires breaking out, not to the point of destroying the house, but certainly infuriating the inhabitants. Such manifestations have been known to continue over a period of months and even years.

Today modern science frequently ignores the occult theories advanced to explain such events as the products of disturbed and emotionally weak personalities, or attribute them to the obsessions of strange fringe cultists and hysterical aging spinsters. Those who know of the existence of organizations attempting scientific investigations of unexplained phenomena think merely of the card games played at Duke University by Dr. Rhine's group. Seldom in the United States is the word *poltergeist* taken seriously.

Like so many English words, *poltergeist* comes from German. The name derives from two common German words: *polter*, to make a hullabaloo or bluster, and *geist*, meaning spirit, wit, mind, genius, or ghost. The well-known writer, Shane Leslie, refers to the poltergeist as

". . . the well-known and ever-evidenced type of the uncanny called poltergeists or ghosts that make noises." These cases have been recorded *"ad nauseam,"* Mr. Leslie says, pointing out that such spirits are "materialistic in most of their symptoms."

Noise-producing spirits, turbulence of sound, and similar disturbances do occur and do repeat themselves, not only in folk tales or in primitive, far-off cultures, but here and today. Phenomena of this type commonly accompany the more advanced supernormal manifestations and are well known, indeed expected, in the circles of spiritism or spiritualism. Regrettably, the same rappings and table turnings are too often the stock in trade of the charlatan spirit mediums who frequently abound in all modern societies. American history is rich in such spirit communications which purportedly come as messages from the "Unseen" or the "Other Side" and invariably are produced as simple numerical sequences through an entranced spirit medium. Psychical investigation has so often proved these allegedly occult manifestations are produced by charlatans that most scientists now refuse to waste time with the occasional unexplained incident.

Following the importing of spiritualism from Europe in the nineteenth century, New York became particularly a source for alleged occult disturbances. Hydesville and Rochester were for a time the center of the spiritualist movement, whose events were later proved to be mostly false, or so most authorities now claim. Despite being frequently discredited by modern science, the area continues to be a mecca for the curious and those so willing to believe and ready to place their almost pathetic faith in any inexplicable occurrences.

It was in such an area that Margaret and Kate Fox and the Weemans became so well known, undergoing soft and insistent bedroom tappings during the long and quiet Victorian nights. Although most investigators consider the Foxes to have been deliberate charlatans their memory still attracts followers among the understanding spiritualists as well as the gullible.

The young Fox sisters mystified their parents by being the center of an alleged spirit's attentions, who made his presence known by unaccountable taps in the rooms. Neighbors were called in to witness the manifestations, and the fame of the girls spread far beyond Hydesville, when it was known that the spirit sent messages through the girls by means of coded raps. Eventually, with the aid of an older sister, the Fox girls became professional mediums and made careers of presenting the phenomena on public stages. Scientists challenged the veracity of the manifestations, although thousands of people believed implicitly that they were true. Nor were the believers particularly dismayed when some years later, the older Margaret Fox after a somewhat checkered career, repudiated her spirit activities by announcing that her career had been complete humbug and fraud, and topped this confession by a public performance in New York in 1888, where she demonstrated that the mysterious rappings that formed the spirit's messages were in fact produced by the big toes of herself and her sister Kate.

In Providence, one Almira Beazeley produced revelations by knocking out coded messages from the spirit world, and, carried away by the flush of success, grew bolder and more sinister in her actions. At length the young woman murdered her own brother to fulfill a prediction. At her trial the murderess, however, confessed that these noisy communications were the products of her own manipulations.

What of poltergeists, however? Do they send messages through their strange, disturbing noises, or do they function perhaps as messengers from other higher spirits beyond? The Catholic Church does not commit itself on the point, reserving judgment. The *Catholic Encyclopedia* ignores the possibilities of such manifestations, merely describing the deceptions and inconsistencies in the phenomena of spiritism, attributing the explanations offered to various nineteenth-century writers. Thus, Stainton Moses in 1872 says that these events are caused by spirits of a lower order which exist disembodied below the plane of humanity. Again, other writers claim that poltergeist mischief is actually the result of demonic invention.

The British Society for Psychical Research has proved for many decades that most poltergeist rappings are, in fact, fraudulent. While these events are generally claimed to be of supernatural origin, perhaps it is their occurrence during the multitude of spiritist seances that has led to their discrediting.

Most churches acknowledge the existence of a supernatural sphere, or rather, the supernatural character of man. The preternatural or supernormal are not easily understood or analyzed; both science and religion admit that the laws governing the natural world are yet to be fully explained, religion being somewhat laggard in this confession. Even the spiritualist churches emphasize the religious aspects of man's nature while they play down the more mediumistic approaches to the possible existence of another world.

Writers such as Mr. Leslie as well as the Jesuit priests Rickaby and Thurston seem to agree with many investigators that poltergeists, as distinguished from communicating personalities of the spirit world, are not the dead. The explanations assume that poltergeists do exist on a subhuman order of spirits. They are spirits of low humor who evidently delight in teasing people and causing rather adolescent mischief around the house. This order of racketing spirits is the chief producer of most spontaneous psychical phenomena, all of which are inexplicable to the residents of the houses where they occur.

It is interesting to note that, at least in cases later proved to be fraudulent, all poltergeist manifestations are remarkably uniform in their nature. They tap and rap, knock on walls and persistently racket around the house. They throw crockery, they hurl pots and pans. Furniture is at their mercy, being almost cheerfully tossed around rooms. Even grand pianos are at their pleasure, and the spirits are reported to have lifted these heavy musical instruments from room to room. They have started many small fires which are usually discovered and put out by their unfortunate hosts. They often disclose their presence in unoccupied beds, waving and fluttering the bedclothes, and have been known to rip away sheets to awaken sleepers.

Poltergeists have been known to follow the victims of their attentions to houses other than those in which they became active. The New England witch trials testified to this fact. Here, as in an overwhelming majority of cases, the victims were young girls on the threshold of adolescence. This is characteristic of poltergeist manifestations. The spirit phenomena center about the persons of the young, who are annoyed with the usual bumps and raps as well as biting, scratching, pinpricks, and constant jabs. While boys are not exempt from poltergeist annoyances, they usually occur around girls, one authority claims, in 95 per cent of all cases.

One famous poltergeist was that which disturbed the household of Reverend Eliakim Phelps in Stratford, Connecticut, in 1850. The family returned from church services on Sunday to find the door open, although they had locked it when leaving, and all of the furniture thrown about the rooms in complete disorder, although nothing was stolen, not even a gold watch left in the open. During the afternoon the family returned to church, but Dr. Phelps remained at home in his study undisturbed. Upon the family's return, more inexplicable pranks were discovered. The family clothing played a part in the mischief, with a nightgown arranged on a bed to represent a corpse in its coffin, and in the kitchen, dresses, skirts, blouses and sheets were arranged as effigies of eleven or twelve women kneeling as if at a prayer service. One report says that in the center of the tableau clothing had been bunched up to form the figure of a dwarf, while another figure was suspended from the ceiling, though how this was accomplished was not stated.

As the disturbances continued, furniture began to move about the house and was badly damaged. An umbrella flew out of a stand, while the fire tongs moved to the center of the floor and danced merrily. Tables and chairs were lifted through the air and lamps found their way to piles of papers and started fires. The oldest Phelps boy suffered greatly from the poltergeist, having his clothing torn and ripped from his body, being hung from a tree, and supposedly once thrown into the cistern. A plated brass candlestick flew from the mantel to the floor, where it was repeatedly beaten against the wood until it broke into pieces. Knives and forks, potatoes and turnips were thrown through the air; mysterious and often obscene scribblings appeared in places. Banging and knocking were also heard in various parts of the house, and often ended in frightening screams. Dr. Phelps was a devout and respected gentleman and, according to Hereward Carrington, was interested in clairvoyance, having treated many illnesses with mesmerism. Far from shunning notice of the affair, Dr. Phelps kept records of the trouble and was completely welcome to investigation.

Along with the spirit that disturbed the Wesleys at Epworth Rectory, the phantom drummer of Tedworth is equally famous. The case is also disputed for much the same reason, that there were no first-hand accounts given by disinterested witnesses. Frank Podmore, who wrote of the affair, states that most of the account comes from Reverend Joseph Glanvil's *Sadducismus Triumphatus* in the third edition seven years after the event, pointing out that Glanvil's narrative was derived from third- to tenth-hand reports.

The drummer of Tedworth appeared in the spring of 1661 when a vagrant was arrested and brought before the magistrate of Tedworth, John Mompesson. Having forged papers in his possession, the drummer was sentenced to jail and his drum confiscated. About a month later the Mompesson household began hearing strange bangings and then the tattoo of drums around the premises. The manifestations continued night after night, accompanied by disgusting, sulphurous smells, the moving of chairs and boots over the floor, clothing strewn about, mysterious lights, and the appearance to a servant of a fearful body with red and glaring eyes.

The Mompesson children were especially bothered, being struck and shaken in their beds, and terrified by the sounds of iron claws scratching the floor. The children were lifted into the air from their beds, and often followed to other rooms.

These troubles continued over two years and caused much consternation in the house. Then it was learned that the vagrant had bragged that he was well-versed in witchcraft and the dark arts and would make the magistrate regret his confiscation of the drum. The vagrant was then tried for witchcraft at Sarum and, escaping hanging, was sentenced to transportation, after which all troubles ceased.

Naturally there is not one exact or specific type of poltergeist; the manifestations vary with those that receive his attentions. Or as some authorities claim, with those who actually cause the incidents, although the reasons for these causes and the actual physical actions demonstrating annoyances are so deeply buried in the subconscious as to be unknown to the person himself. The poltergeist seems, however, to maintain one specific characteristic in all situations. He is heard but rarely seen, reversing the maxim that children should be seen but not heard. And the poltergeist could be considered a child in his behavior, even by those who consider him a purely spirit manifestation, all physical and psychological explanations aside. His behavior is identical to that of the attention-seeking child, the sort of child who is poised emotionally and physically between childhood and adolescence. He will do anything to attract attention, and annoying or plaguing others, especially adults, is the most effective method. He seems to be saying, "Look, here I am, don't ignore me! I want you to notice me!"

The poltergeist of Doarlish Cashen is exceptional, however, since he—or it—assumed a distinct nature, that of an animal, and one that could talk. This manifestation appeared in the house of the Irving family in England, in a lonely farmhouse far from any neighbors on a point of land overlooking the sea. He became famous as Gef, the talking mongoose, and while books have been devoted to him, a few paragraphs can here summarize his career.

The Irvings were a farm family, poor but well respected, consisting of the parents, a twelve-year-old daughter, and a pet sheepdog named Mona. And, of course, Gef. The family lived on the Isle of Man and were known to all as completely honest, truthful people. Then, as now, there was little that could be hidden from neighbors in so sparsely populated a location. Certainly if the Irvings had any tendency toward conscious trickery or a penchant for hoaxes, it would be well known to all of their fellow Manxmen.

Gef, as the spirit was called, was totally unlike the more customary poltergeists, since he did not occupy his time bedevilling the family, throwing stones, knocking on walls, or breaking crockery. Instead, he appeared as an articulate and talkative spirit, whose greatest desire seemed to be to converse with the Irvings. It was reported that he talked at length, sang the current songs, and possessed a consuming interest in all of the neighborhood gossip, which he would then relate to the family after his alleged rambles. And although he was not seen, he apparently left evidence of his existence, since the Irvings had to put out food and water for the beast, and clean up after him; Gef, it seems, was not housebroken.

Naturally, a phenomenon as wonderful as Gef could not be kept secret in so small a place, even though the Irvings did not court publicity in any way. Investigators and interested psychical researchers soon began to visit the lonely farmhouse, and some of them stayed and witnessed the phenomena for weeks, without being able to detect any fraud or trickery. As in similar incidents of poltergeist phenomena the child was the first consideration of the investigators, yet none could trace Gef's activities to the young girl.

Dr. Nandor Fodor, the psychologist, visited the Irving family at the time and, even though he states that he was not then fully versed in psychiatry, casts an interesting light on the appearances of Gef. Dr. Fodor points out that Mr. Irving was not a farmer by upbringing, but had been an unsuccessful salesman and was a man of integrity and also a man of pride. He refused to accept payment from those who came to observe Gef's activities. A man who has failed in his chosen livelihood and retreated to an isolated farm to lick his wounds does not confess to his neighbors his lack of success, least of all to himself. He hides his sense of guilt and represses his feelings of inadequacy. And with these repressions, his emotional outlets, too, are closed off. It could be that Gef was actually a projection of Mr. Irving's repressed personality, his unconscious desire for recognition and attention. Dr. Fodor points out that in his opinion, and by examining the nature of the phenomena, Gef could not be considered a ghost or a poltergeist, nor could he be thought of as a familiar or an animal. He was, after all, never seen.

And there, unfortunately, the story of the talking mongoose, Gef, must end, since shortly after Dr. Fodor's visits the Irving family left Doarlish Cashen and the Isle of Man and vanished, not to be heard of again.

In the well-known case of the Coonian poltergeist all of these phenomena occurred. The Coonian poltergeist began its appearances in County Fermanagh, Ireland, during the years 1913–1914. It was investigated almost a hundred times by several of the neighborhood's priests. The house in which the poltergeist manifested itself had passed through the hands of several families, and it was during the occupancies of the Sherrys and the Murphys that the spirit became active. The wise Sherry family, after a single disturbed night there, fled and kept the matter quiet until the house was later sold to the Murphys.

At first the spirit made itself known in one bedroom of the house. The pillows were whipped from under the heads of the unfortunate Murphy girls while they were trying to sleep. On other occasions the spirit took the forms of snakes, dogs, rats, eels, and humans under the furiously moving sheets of the bed. The room, by then seldom occupied, contained a tester bed normally occupied by three or four girls under eighteen.

The sounds produced by the poltergeist ran the gamut of snoring, moving and swishing straw, a kicking horse, wall knocking as well as tapping of furniture and the cracking of knuckles. Upon occasions it answered questions by rapping out answers in English, Latin, and Gaelic. The spirit's repertoire was reported to include the singing of Irish folk tunes, whistling, and, during

62

one visit, the unpleasant gurgles and choking sounds of a person in his death agonies.

The investigating clergy naturally considered the possibility of the sounds being caused by the children but, when the arms and legs of the girls were held tightly, the noises still continued. It was concluded on two separate occasions that the children could not have produced the ghostly sounds that accompanied the visit of the poltergeist.

Poltergeists are claimed to display an irreverent attitude toward the ceremonies and objects of the Church, and the Irish manifestation followed the customary pattern. Holy water seemed to increase the occult displeasure while the rites of the Latin mass did little to abate the nuisance. Unlike the isolated cases of diabolic possession, the rites of Exorcism were not held for the Coonian poltergeist. The older clergy of the neighborhood, in fact, kept clear of the Murphy household, while the younger priests attempted to rid the place of its problem with whatever spiritual means were available to them.

Nor did the poltergeist confine its noisy persecution to the young girls of the family. One priest thought that possibly the older members of the family were bothered, too, and, when putting his idea to the test, discovered that twenty-year-old Annie Murphy was also the object of the spirit's unwholesome attentions.

The final appearance of the Coonian poltergeist came about during the visit of a priest returning from a sick call to a neighbor. Unknown to the members of the Murphy clan, he took out the Pyx when the lights dimmed and made the sign of the cross with it over the bed. Mr. Leslie writes, "He had no sooner done so than all the noises imaginable were made before the evil spirits departed and did not return . . ." He concludes his account of the phenomena with the firm statement, "It was not a ghost but a poltergeist obsessed by truly Demoniacal powers."

The *Encyclopedia Britannica* seems to agree with the Society for Psychical Research concerning alleged manifestations of poltergeists. Pointing out the remarkable similarities in such cases, the *Britannica* feels that in these matters the presence of a "principal agent" is essential to produce the occult events. The removal of this principal, even though his secondary agent may remain, will almost always slow or stop the strange occurrences. The writer of the article feels that this principal agent is usually a person of "marked physical or mental abnormality" possessed by a craving for notoriety and desiring to create sensation. This agent is most often a girl going into her teens, occasionally a boy of the same age, and an adult only in the rarest examples. The reported cases are characterized by fraud, usually motivated by hysteria, although there remains in other records an "unexplained residue" of causation.

Possibly some of these factors were operative in the Murphy case; the elements of principal agents working with secondary agents certainly appear to be present. Ireland in the early part of this century could, too, have produced many cases of alleged occult phenomena which were actually the result of religious hysteria. Unfortunately, no scientific investigation or examinations of the Murphys was made since Ireland, then as now, preferred the more traditional explanations offered by her accustomed and dominant church. The family was heard of no more after moving to America, so the matter could no further be pursued.

Our modern minds, of course, prefer scientific explanations of any occult happenings ascribed to poltergeists and other spirits. A private detective could easily uncover the sensation-seeking charlatan, while any intelligent college sophomore can today describe the psychological basis of hysteria.

And common sense provides the explanation of any strange sounds around the house, doesn't it?

But listen: did you hear then a bump on the stairway? And who *is* tapping?

CHAPTER SIX

Two Sisters

The year 1848 marks a turning point for those interested in psychical phenomena in America since, according to spiritualist belief, it was the first time that communications between the living and the spirit world were achieved in this country. And the people who accomplished this first intelligent link with the spirits were not practiced adults with well-developed powers of mediumship but two small girls whose simple and devout Methodist upbringing did not even include the possibility of receiving messages from the dead.

In the winter of 1847 a farmer named John Fox brought his family into northern New York state to a farm near the village of Hydesville, about thirty miles from the city of Rochester. His two daughters, Margaret and Katherine, were about twelve and eight years old at the time and lived at home with their parents, while two other children lived not far away. Leah Fox Fish was living then in Rochester with her husband, and David Fox made his home only a few miles from his parents.

The house to which the Fox family moved was said, by

neighbors in Arcadia township, to be haunted, but these rumors did not deter Mr. and Mrs. Fox, who were strict and sincere believers in Methodism. Although northern New York was at that time fertile ground for the growth of emotionally charged cults and self-proclaimed religious prophets, the Foxes were not inclined to put stock in stories that they considered pure superstition. It was true that the family of Michael Weekman had left the house after living there less than two years, but John Fox couldn't take too seriously the reasons given that caused the Weekmans to move, since it was said that the stories were told around by their hired girl.

For the first few months the Foxes lived peacefully in the two-storied wooden farmhouse, undisturbed except by some soft noises that could easily have been caused by mice or even the wind. By early spring, though, these sounds seemed to be bothering the girls and frequently disturbed their sleep. Then, at the end of March, the family heard noises that were not mice gnawing on the walls. Mrs. Fox one night heard the distinct sounds of someone rapping in the house. She went to the room shared by the two girls to see what the trouble was, but the children were apparently sleeping peacefully, even as the tapping continued. Discussion was held the following day, with no results to show what made the noises, and the matter was forgotten until that night when the rapping was heard again. The parents were mystified, since their investigations could not uncover the cause of the sound, nor did the tapping on the next day clear up matters for them.

The neighboring shoemaker was questioned but denied that he ever repaired shoes at night. David Fox, called to the house by his parents, was as baffled by the noises as they were and could offer no reasonable explanations. The windows and doors seemed to be tight within their frames; for that matter the raps were not the random sounds which result from the house being shaken by the wind, but came at positive and definite intervals. Worried that the girls would be frightened by the tapping, and partly wondering if they themselves might be making the sounds, Mrs. Fox ordered the girls the next night to lie quietly in their bed and not to pay any attention to any noises they might hear.

The tapping became louder and more insistent that night, so loud that the girls could not sleep but sat up and called out in surprise. They were less frightened than curious about the mysterious noises, and they quickly accustomed themselves to the nightly disturbances. The two sisters soon realized that whenever their father would test the shutters or the window sashes with a slight push, the taps would answer back as echoes to his efforts. One of the girls—some say Margaret, others claim it was Kate— was enchanted with this new game and called out, clapping her hands together, "Mr. Split-foot, do as I do!" The answering raps echoed the same number that she had given. The girl then asked the spirit to repeat her actions by number, as she pressed one hand against the other four times, and again the spirit responded by tapping in the same sequence.

While the girls were amused by their new playmate, Mrs. Fox was more baffled than ever. According to her signed statement, Mrs. Fox then raised her voice, even though her husband appeared speechless with fright, and asked that the spirit rap the correct ages of the girls.

The raps came back immediately in answer to her questions, as did the rapping that indicated the proper number of children she had borne. Summoning her courage Mrs. Fox then asked if it was a living human who made the sounds, but there was an unresponsive silence. To her question as to whether a spirit made the noises, the raps came back affirmatively.

The question in the minds of the adults was what spirit could be trying to reach the world in this manner. Mrs. Fox, perhaps feeling that some of the longtime residents of the area might know, asked if the spirit would tap if neighbors were present. The spirit rapped back that it would.

Mr. and Mrs. Fox were known as simple, honest country people, uncomplicated and direct in their dealings, and the neighbors must have added gullible to the list of their qualities when told the reason for the invitations. Perhaps they came to mock, but when they heard the spirit rap out answers to questions put to him, the people stayed to wonder. They continued to come back to the Fox house to marvel at the unaccountable performances, and as the number of visitors swelled, the stories were carried far beyond the small village. Some left the house still skeptical, others as confirmed believers; all observers agreed on one fact, though: the spirit seemed to need the presence of Margaret and Kate Fox to provide the medium by which he sent his messages.

During the weeks following the first spirit revelations a decipherable code of rappings was devised, through which the spirit could answer much more detailed inquiries. Raps indicating yes and no were worked out, as well as various systems to indicate letters of the alphabet and numbers, and through this ghostly Morse code the spirit was able to express himself and tell the assembled audience exactly who he was and why he lingered at the spot. There are many conflicting accounts concerning the questioning that followed and who asked the spirit for information, but if Mrs. Fox's statement is to be believed, it was she who asked whether the spirit had been hurt or injured. To his affirmative rap, she asked whether he had been injured in the house. Again the people heard the raps that said yes.

The questioning continued, slowly and with difficulty, but finally a comprehensive picture of the spirit took shape. He rapped out that he had been a thirty-one-year-old peddler who had been murdered in the house for his money while showing his wares to an occupant a few years earlier. His body was secretly buried in the cellar, and he had left a widow and five children behind. His wife he said, was now dead. To those who asked his name, he gave no answer, nor did he agree that Michael Weekman, the previous tenant, committed the crime. His body still lay buried ten feet deep in the cellar.

The men soon went down to the cellar with shovels and spades to unearth, if they could, the ghastly proof of the spirit's claims. Digging and digging uncovered no body or skeleton that could be identified as a man's, but bits and pieces of bones, quicklime, and pottery were found, while some larger bone fragments were thought by some to be part of a human skull.

Other manifestations became apparent in the Fox house after these disclosures, and the family heard more knockings and taps in various parts of the house. The beds were shaken and rocked, cold and clammy hands pulled at the bedclothes, and from the cellar there came the sounds of a death struggle, which ended with strangling noises and then the ominous sound of a heavy object being dragged over the dirt floor. The older Fox daughter from Rochester was visiting the family by now, and it was agreed that to protect the children, Leah would take them with her back to the city.

The spirit followed Margaret and Kate to their older sister's home and continued to make his presence known, both by his raps and by throwing small objects about the rooms. Leah's neighbors soon wanted to witness the spirit's nightly visits, and the house in Rochester also became a mecca for the curious and for the believers who, if some reports are correct, were quite willing to pay for the privilege. The popularity of the demonstrations by the two Fox sisters became so great that sister Leah devoted more and more of her time watching over their interests, and less to the music teaching that earned her living. By then many of the Rochester citizens had withdrawn their children from Leah's tutelage, anyway, because of the notoriety that was beginning to surround the Fox girls. The newspapers, both in that city and all around the country, had featured articles about the spirit phenomena with a sensational approach that made the more conservative Rochester residents criticize the whole affair.

Charges of fraud were starting to circulate concerning the rappings of the spirit and the incidents that were taking place at Leah Fox Fish's house. Some of the more skeptical pointed out that the spirit, if that was what rapped out the messages, only sent communications when the two Fox girls were present and seemed unwilling or unable to manifest itself without them. The clergy of the city, too, were now making their opinions felt on the matter, stating that Margaret and Kate Fox, with the assistance of Leah and other members of the family, were actually calling upon the evil one for assistance in perpetrating a gigantic hoax upon the public. Nothing in the Bible could be found to indicate a scriptural basis for the idea that the spirits of the dead were able to come back and communicate with the living. These notions smacked of the diabolic, and should be treated gingerly, they said.

Kate, the younger of the two girls, was sent away from Rochester for her own welfare, while Margaret remained in her sister's house, but the separation of the two girls did nothing to alleviate the presence of the spirits. The rappings increased and the talk continued. Charges of fraud and vicious slanders were increasing, and some felt that the growing opposition to the girl might endanger her safety.

The situation was reaching a crisis when a group of citizens sprang to the young girl's defense and came together as a group that met nightly in the house to observe the spirit demonstrations. Through these nightly gatherings Margaret's powers were apparently reaching a higher stage of development, and it became plain that spirits other than the murdered peddler were attempting to reach this world. Nor were these spirits, like the peddler, an unhappy ghost who wanted to tell the living of his murder, but were those of people who had died naturally and found happiness in the spirit world. Their purpose was not to seek vengeance but to convince the loved ones left behind of the existence of the hereafter and of their own contentment and happiness, now that they had been relieved of their earthly cares.

While many of Rochester's clergy condemned the demonstrations, others believed in the truth of the manifestations and sought to answer the questions once and for all by holding a public exhibition. Some of the group that had gathered about Margaret thought that this lecture should take place in a church under the leadership of the city's ministers, but when questioned through Margaret, the spirits declared otherwise. The meeting, they said, should be held in a public lecture hall large enough to hold all of the interested citizens as well as the skeptical. Margaret and her family welcomed the idea of a public meeting, and stated that she and Kate were perfectly willing to submit to any questions and investigations that would be made. The mundane details of the lecture were handled by Leah, who arranged for a small contribution to be asked of each member of the audience to defray expenses, while prominent citizens and clergy would form the committee of investigation.

The first public meeting produced inconclusive results, and a second was arranged, with the investigating committee to be chosen from those respectable citizens who had indicated the greater degree of skepticism. None of the witnesses could discern the cause of the rappings, which showered the hall and frequently interrupted the speeches that were being made.

Many of the audience left the second meeting as they had come, skeptical and unconvinced, but others were converted on the spot and took up the cause in defense of the Fox girls and their inexplicable powers to reach the dead. When public clamor reached its peak it was decided that a larger hall would be necessary to accommodate all of those who wanted to see for themselves the spirit marvels. Leah then arranged to show her sisters in New York, and although told to require a large contribution from those admitted to the hall, she refused. She suggested a much lower charge, feeling that this would permit the greatest number of people to see the girls exhibiting their powers of mediumship. The press argued the pros and cons of the lecture series, but the public attended in droves. Many of the leading intellectuals and statesmen of the time came and were fascinated by the girls; some even left convinced of the truth of their claims. Among them was a justice of the state Supreme Court, Judge Edmonds; Horace Greeley, the publisher, showed helpful interest in the seances while preserving an open mind and waiting for further proof.

Steps were taken to prevent the public meetings from assuming a carnival atmosphere, and the audience was requested to join in the hymn singing that began each performance and to maintain as serious and reverent an attitude as possible. The position of spirit influence in religion was developing, which would later result in the formation of the spiritualist churches known today. By arrangement with sister Leah and Mrs. Fox, Margaret also provided private seances conducted in their hotel rooms, to which those seeking reassurance of the existence of the afterlife and personal messages from their loved ones came by appointment.

During the public meetings the girls were observed closely by a group of skeptical physicians who then gave their opinion that the knockings did not come from the spirit world, but were actually produced by physical manipulations of the girl's bodies. The Fox family, through their representatives, challenged this opinion and welcomed further study of the phenomena. Another medical committee was drawn up and Margaret was examined extensively and with the closest scrutiny. Though the young girl's limbs were held tightly by the medical observers, the rappings still sounded in the room.

The appearances of the girls were a resounding success in New York and a national tour was arranged. To these meetings, as in New York, the public came by the thousands, and the audiences included some of the most prominent of America's clergy, professors, and other important professional men and businessmen. The common people also attended to see the wonders and returned to their homes in awe and amazement.

When the tour was completed the Fox family returned to the East Coast. There, young Katherine was taken into his home by Horace Greeley and his wife, who gave her the necessary schooling that she had been missing. Margaret and her mother, though, moved to Philadelphia, where they conducted private seances in their rooms for select groups, some of whom were already initiates, while others attended for the first time. It was at one of these meetings that Margaret met Dr. Elisha Kane, himself a national celebrity.

Dr. Kane was only in his early thirties when he met Margaret, but he had already achieved renown both as a surgeon and as an explorer. His family were of position and substance, living in a Philadelphia suburb, and he was as charming as he was handsome. From the first he was struck by the girl, and quickly took her under his wing, placing her with his family and providing for her education and training in the ladylike arts. The attachment between the sophisticated doctor and the young medium grew, and she returned his affection.

Dr. Kane's health had been impaired by an ill-fated voyage of exploration to the Arctic regions, and after some years watching over Margaret, it was suggested that he might improve physically by travelling abroad. Neither welcomed the separation, and before setting sail Dr. Kane and Margaret Fox were married in a private ceremony which consisted of simple declaration by the doctor of his intent. Travelling, unfortunately, did nothing for Dr. Kane's condition, and his health steadily deteriorated until, in Cuba in 1857. he died. When the news reached Margaret and her mother, the girl collapsed. She had been truly devoted to the Philadelphia aristocrat who was both husband and father to her, and for months she lay sick. And matters were not helped by the disclosure that, although Dr. Kane intended to leave a substantial estate to Margaret, his family would not recognize her as his widow since no religious or civil ceremony had ever taken place. Finally after considerable wrangling, the Kane family did agree to give Margaret a pittance, but by then it was clear that she would be forced to continue giving seances to make ends meet.

And so Margaret Fox's long and sad journey began, which took her for almost forty years back and forth over the country and abroad. Life grew increasingly difficult for her, and her presence on the lecture platforms no longer drew the crowds it once had. Hundreds of spirit mediums had begun conducting meetings and seances, many of whom could only be described as deliberate charlatans, and by sleight of hand and trickery were producing quick and spectacular messages and manifestations from the spirit world. Mrs. Kane, as Margaret now called herself, found that earning her livelihood through public mediumship was a growing hardship. Perhaps she also felt remorse for following this course against Dr. Kane's wishes, since she had promised him that she would give up spirit demonstrations and seances. Alone now, and poor, she found her solace in the Catholic Church and her comfort in the bottle.

In 1888 when she returned from a stay in England Margaret gave an interview to the press in which she said that she was sickened by the fraud that attached itself to spiritualism and promised to expose the hoax. Shortly afterward another interview appeared, this one given by Kate Fox, in which she concurred with Margaret's statements.

The publication of these interviews created a furor. The idea of statements such as these made by the very founders of spiritualism filled the hearts of the believers with dismay. Many attributed the interviews to the well-known drinking habits of Mrs. Kane, while skeptics were the first to say, I told you so.

On October 21st the Academy of Music in New York held a standing-room-only crowd. Many were ardent spiritualists who did not want to believe the claims of fraud, while others were there merely in the hope of seeing a sensation—and they were not disappointed.

Margaret proceeded rather nervously to read a statement in which she confessed that the rappings which began in the farmhouse at Hydesville were a total fraud. She added that the greatest shame of her life was continuing to foist this hoax on the innocent and harmless public. The original rappings were done out of childish mischief to frighten their simple and good-hearted mother as a prank. And then, with her shoe removed, Margaret proceeded to demonstrate exactly how they had produced the knocking. With her foot resting on a thin pine table she began to flex and crack her big toe, and the hall was filled with the sounds of knockings.

Margaret Fox died in Brooklyn in 1893, after a briefly successful tour of exposing spirit rappings and then a futile return to conducting seances. In her public confession five years earlier she told in detail exactly how the spirit rappings were produced and how her family helped her to produce the proper answers to questions. And yet it has been written that her funeral was attended by many faithful and practicing spiritualists who followed her coffin to the cemetery and saw her lowered to her grave.

CHAPTER SEVEN

The Bell Witch

There are probably times when at family gatherings you might wonder just what to say to the older members of the family. Life moves at such a fast pace today that it becomes increasingly difficult for the generations to bridge the gap and communicate. The young have their future, while the old only their memories, and these hold little interest for their grandchildren. Yet it might be worthwhile for the younger generation to take time to sit down and listen to their elders. They might hear stories of the earlier days that could startle them.

Consider Betsy Bell, who was born about 1805, still hearty and well in her eighties. Her stories of her childhood back in Tennessee are far from the ordinary talk of farm life. She could tell of strange and wonderful happenings, and talk of witchcraft and hauntings and finally murder in tones to chill the blood. They would be true stories, too, and she was the center of the horrible events that make up the story of the Bell Witch.

Betsy Bell was one of five children of John and Luce Bell, who farmed in Robertson County, Tennessee, in the north of the state above Nashville. She was the only girl; two boys, John Jr. and Drewry, were older, and Joel and Richard William were younger. John was twelve years older than Betsy and was her favorite brother; she idolized him just as she did her mother, Luce. The other boys? Well, they were brothers, and can be a bother to the only girl. Her father must have been stern and hard-bitten; she didn't feel toward him what she did for her mother. But then this is often true of children; they respect one parent, and worship the other.

Betsy was twelve when the witch came to the Bells, and sixteen when she left them, and those four years mark the difference between a child and a woman, especially in the backwoods country of pioneer America. After those four years she had lost her father, had her romance broken, and suffered torments and persecutions from unseen hands that would age a stronger person in a later era.

The first signs of the troubles began in 1817, in the early evening when the family were all together in the farm house after supper. This was always the time of day that farm people met, after the day's work was done—and it could be backbreaking work in the early 1800's—when supper was finished and the dishes cleared away. This was the time when they could talk easily, play a few games, crack jokes, and enjoy each others' company. There were serious moments, of course; this was God-fearing country, and probably the Bell family listened to the father, John Bell, read several chapters from the Bible every night, as did most of the families in that part of the country.

Younger children, naturally, could be restless while the

reading from the Scriptures went on too long, with all the names of the Old Testament Kings and Prophets to try to remember. Sometimes they might be a little too high spirited, teasing each other and playing pranks when their elders weren't watching. So when the knocking and scratching started that night in the Bell farm house, old John Bell must have looked up from the Book and blamed it on one of the children. They protested that they didn't do it, because the knocking and the scratching were on the outside of the doors and the windows. Usually a fierce glare and a sharp reprimand would put a stop to nonsense of this sort, but the children were right this time.

The tapping, the knocking, the strange scraping sounds still continued, not only that first night, but the night after, and the one after that. And so it went for some weeks, every night, and the children were as bewildered as their parents as to who was making the noises. Bewildered and a little frightened, too, since by now the parents were completely puzzled and unable to make it out.

Then the noises moved inside and came from the bedrooms and the floors and the walls. Now the sounds were more than simple knocking on the walls, although that still happened. The irritating noises made by a rat gnawing on wood were heard during the long nights, and the scraping of the claws of a hound on the floor, over and over, but nothing could be seen even though the family searched every corner of the house to find the rat or the dog. Before the family could determine the reasons for these disturbances, more noises were added. The splintering of wood as if the bedsteads were being pulled apart by invisible hands was heard, and then the snarling of a dog-fight, until the family was at a loss to locate the cause of these wonders. The noises and sounds then became human, and strangling, choking noises seemed to come from all corners of the house. The Bells did their best to find the reason for these troubles, but whenever they went to investigate, the noises would stop, and then begin in another part of the house. In spite of all their efforts to locate the source of the unfathomable sounds, the Bells were baffled and unsuccessful. Nothing could be discovered to explain the mysterious noises, nor could the blame be laid to any of the children.

A neighbor, Mr. Johnson, was called to the farm, and the whole story laid before him, hoping that he could help them unearth the cause of the disturbances. He listened to the noises in amazement and then gave as his opinion that the cause was an intelligent spirit, since the sounds stopped temporarily when the name of the Lord was invoked. He suggested bringing more of the neighbors to hear these wonders, on the theory that other opinions might be helpful in solving the mystery.

Yet the neighbors could not discover what was causing the trouble, either, even though they were able to watch every member of the Bell family closely. The noises increased, and now it could be seen that the spirit's attention was directed toward young Betsy Bell. Her cheeks would suddenly turn red, as though she had been slapped sharply in the face, and she suffered the same pain that would have resulted from a blow by a visible human being. Even sending Betsy out of the house to the neighbors for her protection didn't help; the invisible spirit followed her wherever she went, slapping and pinching her, and surrounding her with the constant strange racket.

And now the spirit at the Bell house could no longer be kept a secret within the family, and the homestead became a sensation in Robertson County. Every night the house was filled with people wanting to hear about the spirit and hear for themselves the mysterious noises. The witch obliged the visitors, rapping the walls at their request, and making the odd human sounds of gurgling, sighing, and whistling.

It seemed that the spirit was able now to do more than rap on the windows and sigh. It could throw stones and pieces of wood, and did at the younger boys when they were walking through the woods near the farm. Even in the house it seemed to take delight in frightening the boys; young Richard was terrified one night when the spirit woke him by pulling his hair furiously, almost dragging him from the bed. His brother cried out in alarm, but before the parents could find out the cause, they heard Betsy begin to scream and cry from her own room that the spirit was pulling her hair vigorously.

As the power of the spirit to make noises grew, so did its power to hurt the children, and the beatings and pinchings became more vicious as the weeks passed. But by now there was more than this to amaze the countryside. What had been gurgling and choking sounds changed, and the spirit was now whistling softly and whispering. At first the whispers were low and barely able to hear, but they grew louder and the listeners realized that the spirit was talking to them. The words were difficult to understand when the whispering began, but as time passed words and whole sentences became clear.

Now the Bells knew what was afflicting them, when the spirit was able to talk clearly and tell them, "I am a

Spirit from everywhere, Heaven, Hell, the Earth; am in the air, in houses, any place at any time, have been created millions of years; that is all I will tell you." What spirit could this be? The low sibilance answered their questions, saying that she was the spirit of old Kate Batts, come back to take her revenge of John Bell and his family because he cheated her when they did business. She had said that she would get even with John Bell if she had to even after her death, and she would torment him into his grave.

By this time Betsy Bell was suffering greatly from the witch's presence, having fainting spells and trouble with her breathing. Sometimes she felt as if she was going to smother, then she would pant and choke, then become exhausted. Her spells grew so severe that she would at length become unconscious, and couldn't be revived for almost an hour. Betsy's spells always came in the evenings, at the same time the witch came to torment the family, and she would faint and lie unconscious all the while the witch screamed and swore at her father. When the witch finally became silent Betsy could be revived, and after her quick recovery, showed no physical signs of having these terrible and exhausting spells.

When the witch affirmed that she was the spirit of Kate Batts and Betsy's seizures began, John Bell began his long siege of afflictions. He began feeling strange and uncomfortable sensations in his mouth, as if his tongue was growing stiff in his mouth and then swelling so that he was neither able to eat nor to talk for hours on end. He told the family that he could feel something like a stick across his mouth, punching each side of his jaws painfully. And then he started to develop facial contortions and uncontrollable tics, and these troubles prevented him from talking when they seized him.

It was said in family accounts that when John Bell's afflictions began troubling him, his daughter Betsy's became less severe until they finally disappeared. But the witch remained to see the father's sufferings, and throughout his pain her invisible voice could be heard shouting and ranting against him, calling him vile names, making the house ring with her blasphemies, and calling for his death.

With the other members of the Bell family, though, the witch acted and spoke in a different manner. She began to speak piously and present her unseen self as a devout, Bible-quoting creature, and frequently would sing hymns beautifully and quote sermons that the preachers had delivered on the previous Sundays. She was able even to imitate the ministers' voices, as well as produce passable mockeries of the voices of John Bell and others.

Toward Mrs. Bell the witch displayed great tenderness and affection, announcing that she was one of the finest women who lived, though still continuing the spectral torments of her husband and children. And when Mrs. Bell became ill and took to her bed, undoubtedly as a result of the tribulations inflicted on the family, the witch spoke in sorrowful tones to the poor woman. As if contrite, she offered her gifts of fruit and nuts which dropped onto Mrs. Bell's bed, and even cracked the nuts when the woman was unable to do so herself.

Even though the witch displayed great worry over Mrs. Bell's illness and inquired plaintively how the woman felt, she was not able to heal her, nor did she make any claims that she could produce supernatural healing and cure sicknesses.

The occult gifts of fruit and nuts were on several occasions witnessed by neighbor women who were visiting Mrs. Bell, and amazed all beholders. They searched the room above Mrs. Bell's bedroom, since the nuts fell from the air to the bed, thinking that someone might have dropped them through cracks in the floorboards, but when the rugs were rolled back no cracks could be found and nobody could offer an explanation as to how the gifts were brought.

Even more strange were the fruit and nuts brought to Mrs. Bell's Bible group when it met at the farm house when she was well. After the study of the Scriptures was over, it was usual for the hostess to offer refreshments to the visitors, and the witch followed the country customs. Before the bewildered eyes of the ladies, fruit and nuts came out of the air and dropped onto the table and in their laps, while the ghostly disembodied voice invited them to eat and enjoy their meal. Moreover, it was said that these were not any fruits to be found in Tennessee in those days, but oranges, grapes, and bananas which the witch said that she had brought all the way from the West Indies.

The witch's greatest hatred was directed at father Bell, while her strongest affection seems to have been shown to his wife. But the witch also spared John, Jr., from her malicious torments and, though teasing and occasionally beating the younger boys, once saved the life of one of their friends. The boys, along with Betsy, were exploring the recesses of a nearby cave when one tripped and fell into a bed of quicksand. Though the boy's candle went

86

out, the witch promised to save him and suddenly an unaccountable light filled the cave, while tremendously strong and invisible hands pulled him to safety.

The witch was never seen by any of the family or the neighborhood, but she could be felt, as those who suffered beatings and pinchings from her could testify. Sometimes her touch was gentle, too, and was described as soft and velvety when felt. That she was strong there was no question; according to one legend about the Bell witch, she once pulled Betsy and some friends in a sleigh around the house three times, and at so great a speed that the girls had all they could do to keep from falling out when the sleigh cornered the building.

In general, however, the witch continued showing her animosity toward Betsy, just as she continued to threaten and harass her father. The witch became especially upset when it was known that Betsy was engaged to be married to a neighboring boy, Joshua Gardner. The match was considered a good one by everybody in the area, and Joshua Gardner a perfect catch for any girl in Robertson County, except by the witch. At first she pleaded in her low, soft tones for Betsy to forget Joshua and break the engagement, telling the girl that she would have no peace and happiness with the boy, but when the girl persisted in the engagement, the witch grew angry and turned nasty toward Betsy. She started to beat the girl again, pulling and mussing up her hair, sticking pins into her, pinching and bruising her in the most painful manner, and persistently attempting to wear the girl's determination down and break her willful obstinance. The witch's plaintive voice was constantly heard saying, "Please Betsy Bell, don't have Joshua Gardner, please, Betsy Bell, don't marry

Joshua Gardner . . ." as one of the Bell family later wrote. The witch then started to scandalize her listeners by telling all sorts of lurid tales of the engaged couple's behavior, and casting doubts about Betsy's virtue and modesty, until finally the poor girl could hold out no longer. She gave back the ring to Gardner, feeling that if she ever married him, the witch would make every moment of their married life a constant plague.

The ghostly attacks on John Bell were becoming stronger and more virulent as the months passed. The spells when his tongue and face would swell to the point where he could neither talk nor eat lasted now for days, not a few hours as they had in the beginning. The witch alternated with obscene and blasphemous cursing, and then with deadly and ominous threats against the poor man's life. His facial muscles were constantly out of control, and both in the house and out on the farm he would feel the punches and blows from the witch. He would be seized by terrifying convulsions of the face and then of the body, so severe that his shoes would fly from his feet, even though they would be tied on tightly. Even when he became so sick that he was forced to remain in bed, the witch refused to show any mercy, and he lay as a captive to her malice.

By the winter of 1820 John Bell was a whipped and beaten man. He went back to his bed as if knowing he was doomed and unwilling, or unable, to resist and fight any longer. His health declined rapidly in spite of the efforts of the doctors, and it looked as though the witch's threats to harass him to his grave would come true. Then on a cold and bleak December morning shortly before Christmas the family found him lying in a stupor. They tried to bring him around, but could not. The doctor had left medicine for him, and one of the Bell sons thought that possibly a few drops of this clear liquid would turn the tide and rouse him. But the medicine that the doctor had left was not in the cupboard; in its place they found what one of the family wrote of as being "a smoky looking vial, which was about one-third full of a dark colored liquid." The doctor was sent for and while the family waited, they heard the witch shouting, "It's useless for you to try to relieve Old Jack. I have got him this time, he will never get up from that bed again."

When the doctor arrived he was bewildered about the strange-looking medicine that the family found. It certainly wasn't what he had left for John Bell, and he wondered what it could be and where it came from. The witch answered his question: "I put it there, and gave Old Jack a big dose out of it last night while he was fast asleep, which fixed him." The doctor and the family feared the worst from the witch's gloating statement, and tested the unknown fluid on the family cat. They dipped a broomstraw into the bottle and then drew it through the cat's mouth, at which the cat immediately went into violent convulsions and died on the spot.

John Bell lasted a little longer than the cat, but soon sank deeper and deeper into his final coma, while the witch sang and shouted triumphantly over her victim's dying body. After his death the doctor wondered as to the nature of the poisonous liquid and asked for the bottle, but someone had thrown it into the fireplace and it was smashed and all traces of the poison had disappeared. Nobody present seemed to question the witch's claim that she had poisoned John Bell, or wonder why she used this method after demonstrating her great strength for a period of almost four years; it would have been as easy to crush him in his bed. For that matter, it was clear that he would soon have died a natural death, but the witch apparently couldn't wait, and had to vent her last final spite toward him.

Nor did she permit the Bell family to bury their husband and father in peace and dignity but horrified the mourners by her gloating screams and ribald songs throughout the burial ceremony and then back at the farmhouse when neighbors came to pay their respects.

With John Bell gone the witch had lost her chief victim and the reason for her persecutions of the Bell family, and her tormentings became less and less frequent, losing their power and force. Later in the spring as the intensity of the annoyances waned, the witch gave her last message to the Bells, telling them in a soft voice that she was leaving them though she would again return in seven years, and one hundred years after that.

Much has been written about the Bell witch, whose appearances became famous throughout Tennessee and beyond, even when she was appearing. Some believed her to be a truly evil spirit, able to practice her witchcraft even after death, while others claimed that fraud was the basis for all of the stories, and that the Bell family were the cause, especially Betsy. Legends grew up surrounding the hauntings of the Bells and some were so wild and exaggerated that about thirty years later Richard Williams Bell wrote of the affair, not for publication, but to clarify the stories for the other members of the family. Richard Bell's account, however, was not published until almost the end of the century, and includes the quotations of the statements of the witch that are presented here. Another member of the Bell family wrote of the hauntings, too, in the 1930's, basing his narrative in part on conversations held with his great-aunt Betsy when he was a young boy.

Accounts of the Bell witch vary, naturally, since there were no eyewitness records given at the time. Richard, who wrote his diary of the incidents for the family, could not be considered too competent as to the truth of the hauntings, since he was the youngest Bell child, little more than six or seven at the time. Other stories of the Bell witch, of course, reflect the personal points of view of the writers; the professional skeptic naturally attributes the whole mystery to deliberate, conscious fraud on the part of Betsy Bell and others of the family, while the more ingenuous completely believe in the occult explanations and consider no others. Any psychiatrist could find the story of the Bell hauntings a goldmine of source material on abnormal psychology, offering classic examples of guilt repressions and personality dissociation. Other explanations present themselves; perhaps Betsy Bell was a self-taught ventriloquist and the witch's utterances actually came from Betsy's lips. And her seizures during the early weeks of the witch's appearance sound remarkably like the stages in a trance development by a medium.

Whatever the true causes and reasons for the Bell witch and her actions, we will never know. By now the tale is encrusted with legend and romantic exaggeration, becoming part of our American folklore. Perhaps this is for the best, since the actual explanations might be too grim or disillusioning for our tastes. Betsy Bell, her father tormented to his grave, and the Bell witch are by now best understood as legend.

CHAPTER EIGHT

A Walk into the Past

The day began as a clear and warm August day, almost
sultry in fact, but this could be expected of Paris in the
summer. The two Englishwomen had walked endlessly
through the long hallways and great rooms of Versailles,
trudged through the galleries with Baedeckers in hand,
dutifully admiring the magnificence of an earlier era as
tourists, particularly schoolteachers, should. Now they sat
in the *Salle des Glaces* and rested, their long, heavy skirts
clinging oppressively in the heat. Outside the sky had
grown overcast, but Miss Moberly felt a cooling breeze
touch her face and thought how pleasant a stroll through
the gardens would be in the fresh air. Her friend, Miss
Jourdain, agreed; even though she had been to Paris before
she hadn't visited Versailles, and as a person of French
ancestry she felt that she shouldn't miss any of the beauty
of the royal retreat.

The Petit Trianon, Miss Moberly suggested? Of course,
Miss Jourdain agreed. It would be delightful to stroll
through the gardens surrounding the hapless Queen's toy
country house. How charming the grounds must have

looked when Marie Antoinette and the courtiers played at being simple farmers and peasants as a relief from the tedium and rigid magnificence of the court.

The ladies walked out past the fountains and down the great staircase, thankful at least that they were dressed in the sensible styles of 1901 and didn't have to cope with the unwieldy crinolines of their mothers' generation. Down the steps they went to the pond, where they paused for a moment and considered seeing the Grand Trianon, but decided against it. They turned right and walked on toward the Petit Trianon and the English gardens, so designed to create the illusion in a small area of a large, parklike estate.

The two ladies came to a broad drive, and Miss Moberly thought that this must be the way to the Petit Trianon, but her companion continued across the drive and forward along a grassy lane. She had, after all, been to France before and must know the correct way; that must be why she didn't ask directions from the woman shaking a dust-cloth from the window of the nearby building, Miss Moberly thought. Of course she could check in the guide-book, but they had followed the book too faithfully for most of the afternoon. It was pleasant now merely to stroll and wander the grounds without turning the pages of the book.

They followed the lane to the right, passing several buildings, but none were the one they sought. The open door of one building showed that it was deserted, and surely they would find the Petit Trianon crowded with fellow tourists. Ahead of them were three paths winding through the grove of trees, a difficult choice for the women to make, since neither had been to Versailles before.

Fortunately they saw two men standing in the center path, chatting. From the wheelbarrow and the spades by their side, the men could be gardeners, yet something in their bearing made them appear to be officials of some sort. But what strange costumes they wore, long fitted coats of a gray-green color, and their hats were the tricorns of an earlier age. Miss Jourdain wondered, when she asked the men for directions, if the government insisted that the employees at Versailles wear the costumes of Revolutionary times; possibly this could account for the two women on the stone steps of the nearby cottage who wore full skirts, white caps, and kerchiefs tucked into the bodice. Or possibly a pageant was taking place in the gardens later; the women seemed almost to be posing or rehearsing in the manner they handled the country styled jug.

They thanked the officials and took the center path as directed. The skies were leaden with the overcast now, and seemed to bring an extraordinary sense of depression to Miss Moberly. She wondered if her friend felt the same, but didn't want to ask. An uncanny feeling of lethargy crept over her as they walked along the path, and the breeze had died down. Really, the gardens hadn't at all the light and frivolous Watteau charm that she expected, but were entirely different, having an unnatural air of mystery about them.

At last the path ended where another path crossed it. The two teachers stopped and stared ahead. Here the trees were close together, creating the effect of a forest, crowding to the edge of the strange little kiosk that stood in their midst. How strange that a tiny belvedere of this sort should be placed in the grove of trees, with no view whatever; perhaps it once served as a bandstand, Miss Jourdain thought.

They looked about them and then noticed the man sitting near the bandstand. Suddenly both women found their gaze fixed on the figure. He sat completely still, as still as the afternoon had become, in profile to them, his swarthy face shaded by a soft, wide-brimmed hat, and wrapped in a full, dark cloak. The scene before them was almost like an old, tattered tapestry; no sun or shadow beneath the dull sky, not a breath of wind, no leaves stirring or birds singing. All was still, unnaturally so, and unpleasant, as deadly quiet as the man before them.

Then the man turned his head toward them, and both women felt a shiver of revulsion as they saw his face. His dark, pock-marked skin was as repulsive as his staring eyes as he faced them, with a distinctly evil expression although his eyes were unseeing. They stood stock still, frozen by his repugnant, evil face, until the sounds of a man calling behind them broke the spell.

The newcomer called out to the ladies in French, but in so strange an accent they could understand little of what he said. "Ladies," he seemed to be saying, "don't go that way! Here is the way to find the house!" The man ran on into the woods, and the two women were bemused by his strange dress; long, curling hair topped by another wide-brimmed soft hat, a long and dark cloak wrapped around him, and the buckles of his shoes flashing as he disappeared into the trees. As they followed the path he had indicated they heard his footsteps following along with them, although they could see nothing of the man, not even the ancient buckled shoes.

The road led to the right over a tiny country bridge arching above a narrow stream, then along a tree-lined meadow which ended at a house. The house was edged with an English styled garden and had a broad terrace fronting on two sides. Miss Moberly was surprised to see a woman sitting at the edge of the terrace holding out a piece of sketching paper at arm's length. As they walked up to the terrace the woman took no notice of their presence, but squinted at the paper as if she was judging her work. And what a strange costume to wear when sketching, Miss Moberly thought. Although neither young nor attractive, the woman wore a full skirt topped by a pale green fichu, and a wide white hat on her head; hardly the costume for a day sketching in the country, especially on so still and oppressive an afternoon.

On the terrace they stopped and looked around in indecision. There seemed to be no other tourists about, and no doors were open to show them that they were at the proper entrance. Then a young man appeared from the second building along the terrace, slamming the door behind him and breaking the uncanny atmosphere of the day, as he offered to show them the way into the Petit Trianon through the Cour d'Honneur.

At the proper entrance to the Petit Trianon, after following the youth's directions, they found themselves joining a lively, chattering group of tourists which proved to be a wedding party, and continued the rest of the tour without event. Later, taking tea at a hotel near Versailles, both seemed relieved that the day's visit was ended and that they would soon be back into the bustle of Paris.

Miss Moberly felt that the visit to Versailles had been altogether a strange affair and, a week later while writing to a friend, she felt the earlier sense of depression creep over her as she tried to describe that day in her letter. Neither woman had wanted to discuss their trip to Versailles after that afternoon, yet now Miss Moberly felt that she should bring up the matter to her companion. Had Miss Jourdain felt something odd about their day at Versailles, not in the palace but in the gardens of the Petit Trianon? Odd and not natural? Frankly, she asked, did Miss Jourdain feel that the gardens were haunted?

She hesitated about using the word "haunted" since it smacked of the supernatural, and she was sure that Miss Jourdain shared her aversion to anything connected with the occult. But there was no other word to describe her feelings. To her relief Miss Jourdain didn't laugh, but soberly agreed with her own opinion of their strange outing. Yes, she too had experienced the same feeling of oppression during the walk, and amazement at the oddly clothed people they had seen; the behavior of the men and women that afternoon was as out of place as the eighteenth century costumes they wore. And that man who ran to them and insisted that they take the one path and avoid the other. The sound of his running so near to them, yet always out of sight, was certainly uncanny. In all, it had been a rather unpleasant experience that afternoon of the tenth of August, and both ladies then put it from their thoughts after the brief conversation.

In England that autumn both Miss Moberly and Miss Jourdain were too busy with the schedules and the routine of the new school term at Oxford to think back on that mysterious day at Versailles. Miss Jourdain's preparation for her lectures in French and Miss Moberly's duties as principal of St. Hugh's College were more than enough to fill their schedule. It wasn't until November that the two women got together and reminisced about their trip the previous summer. And again the talk turned to that afternoon at the Petit Trianon. There was so much of that walk in the gardens that neither could understand alone; perhaps the other might be able to explain. The woman with the green fichu and the wide, white hat, could Miss Jourdain explain her odd behavior? But no, Miss Jourdain hadn't seen the woman sketching by the terrace, even though they both walked past her. What then of the two women at the steps of the cottage, the older handing a jug to the younger girl—why were they in the dress of an earlier day, could Miss Moberly say? But unfortunately Miss Moberly hadn't seen either of the women.

And so the word "haunted" was spoken again, at first timidly and with a certain diffidence. And then each said what neither had wanted to admit to the other. They were both sensitives and psychic. It had not been the heat and the heavy, overcast skies that depressed them so at Versailles, it was the atmosphere of the gardens themselves. Each had felt the same psychic awareness of something uncanny and unnatural during their walk. Miss Moberly admitted that she had often felt this same awareness in other situations, but didn't care to pursue the matter further. Like so many Scots, both her mother and grandmother talked of their visionary powers and of having second sight while she, after all, was the seventh daughter. But to her this whole idea seemed superstitious, hardly befitting a daughter of the Bishop of Salisbury, and a woman of position and trust at her school.

Miss Jourdain, too, had shied from thinking of her own psychic powers and had avoided any attempt to develop her sensitivity to any higher degree. Dabbling in such matters was more for the ignorant and the foolish and hardly the concern of a supposedly cultivated and intelligent Oxford lecturer.

Still there was so much that neither could explain to herself or to the other. Why hadn't they both seen the same people and noticed the same details of the gardens and the buildings? They then agreed to write a narrative of that August afternoon, independently, and compare their impressions. And if they could not still explain their experiences, perhaps the Society for Psychical Research could cast some light on the matter.

When comparing their independent narratives they found that in general the accounts agreed. Both mentioned the same buildings and details of the gardens, the same oddly dressed people they had encountered, and the same strange conversations held with the peculiar people. There were a few discrepancies, however, the same that they had discussed earlier in Paris. Some people Miss Moberly had seen while Miss Jourdain had not, while Miss Jourdain's narrative spoke of things that had escaped her companion. But in general their memories of the day agreed, so they forwarded their narratives to the S.P.R. in London.

Early in January, 1902, Miss Jourdain found herself in Paris again and, still disturbed by the events of the previous summer, set out on a cold, wet day for Versailles, determined to solve the mystery of the gardens if she could. Ignoring the palace, she set out directly for the Petit Trianon, passing certain buildings she had seen in August. When approaching the artificially laid out country part of the gardens, she felt the familiar cloud of depression settle over her, almost as if she was crossing the boundaries of an unknown land. Looking around her, she saw two laborers piling wood into a cart, both men again dressed in ancient costumes of tunics, capes, and pointed hoods, one red and the other blue. She looked away, then back again, only to find that the men and the cart had disappeared. The landscape now seemed entirely different to her, much more open, and she walked on, away from the buildings, down a confusing network of paths.

Suddenly she saw the man wrapped in a dark cloak to whom she had spoken in August, again gliding in and out of the forest. She puzzled over this odd appearance, but before she was able to speak to the figure, she heard the footsteps of people behind her, with the rustling of heavy, silk skirts coming up the path. There was nobody on the path or anywhere she could see, yet she heard the crowd pressing toward her, surrounding her, the rustle of clothing, and the sounds of voices muttering and whispering to each other. It was as if she was being pressed forward by the invisible mob which then dissipated as mysteriously as it had come.

From the distant woods the sound of music came to Miss Jourdain, who was by now thoroughly bewildered. Faintly she heard band music drifting through the trees, tantalizing scraps of melody that seemed so familiar, but also somehow different. She did her best to keep the melodies in mind, since she had always had an interest in musical theory and harmony, and managed to memorize about twelve bars of the unusual music before the sounds faded away. She felt herself thoroughly lost on the paths now, and tried to follow the map she had brought with her, but whenever she set out on a path that seemed correct she felt herself impelled toward an entirely different one. Finally she sought help from a gardener she encountered and, following his directions, came at last to the Petit Trianon again. As before, the air of gloom lifted as she joined a group of sightseers entering the building.

In the summer of 1904 Miss Jourdain and Miss Moberly went back to Versailles together. Miss Jourdain had told her friend of the completely different appearance of the grounds in January, and together they wanted to revisit the gardens to see if their memories were playing them tricks. In their written narratives they had described the gardens as they first saw them to the best of their abilities, but they wanted to verify Miss Jourdain's impressions from her second visit. She was correct; the grounds and the gardens were different from what they remembered. There were so many changes. There were no deep woods behind a bandstand, nor could they find the bandstand at all. The cottage where the two quaintly dressed women stood with the jug was no longer there, nor the tiny bridge over the stream. Where they had seen the lady sketching by the terrace before, they now found fully grown shrubbery, and the door that the youth had slammed was now locked and cobwebbed, nor had it ever been opened that anyone could remember. They tried to retrace their steps but found that the paths where they had seen the costumed people did not exist. Nor did they see any people in fancy dress; instead, all of the holiday crowds wore contemporary styles, their shouts and laughter filling the air, which was entirely unlike the gloomy quiet and stillness they had felt in 1901.

The two Englishwomen were amazed, both with the different character of the park and gardens, and at the way it verified the notion now growing on them, an idea that was the last from their minds three years earlier. Despite their individual objections to anything that might be considered psychical or supernormal, they could find no rational explanation for the events they had experienced. But there must be a natural reason for the changes in the gardens of the Petit Trianon.

They sought in the archives and libraries the old plans and documents concerning Versailles and the surroundings; here, perhaps, they would find proof that the gardens in 1789 were the same in design as those they saw in 1904 on their second visit. This would prove to their satisfaction that their unfamiliarity with Versailles on their first 1901 trip caused them to make incorrect assumptions about what they saw. To their surprise, however, the opposite theory proved to be correct. What they remembered seeing in 1901, or what they thought they had seen, coincided with the original plans of the gardens of the Petit Trianon as the old documents and plans proved.

They continued their studies of Versailles with sketches, maps, accounts of gardeners, lists of equipment, costume engravings, and all the pertinent documentation they could find, and their researches continued for several years, until they themselves were convinced that their first visit in 1901 constituted a supernormal experience. Finally they brought together the results of their research and together wrote a book-length narrative which in 1911 was published under the title, *An Adventure*. The book was published under pseudonyms to avoid the unpleasantness and ridicule that reward such stories usually and to protect the authors from any notoriety—these were women of position and authority, after all. Miss Moberly used the name Elizabeth Morison, while Miss Jourdain became Frances Lamont.

Among the points cited by the authors in favor of their having experienced the supernormal at Versailles in 1901 were the costumes worn and some of the tools and handicrafts seen. For example, the spade-like hand plow that stood next to the officials they had met could not be found in current use at Versailles. A list of the effects of the King sold after the Revolution, however, recorded a similar implement, and an early engraving depicted a hand plow with an almost identical blade.

Prints and engravings from the time of the Revolution showed both the tricorn and the soft, wide-brimmed hat being worn by men of the time, with the tricorn going out of fashion. Neither the three-cornered hat nor the long coats of the officials had been worn since the Revolution. The other costumes—the cloaks of the men, the wide, full skirts and fichus of the women—were obviously of an earlier day and would, in 1901, be worn only as part of a pageant or play, or possibly a masquerade ball. None of these were taking place at Versailles on the tenth of August that year.

Both of the women had been given a thorough grounding in music, and shared the interests of educated amateurs in harmony. Neither could recognize the twelve bars of music that Miss Jourdain had memorized in 1902, yet the themes seemed tantalizingly familiar. A study of the music libraries in Paris, and the opinions of musicologists and historians indicated that the fragments of music written were not a single theme, but represented several light operatic themes popular about 1780.

The plans of earlier landscape architects and designers seemed to indicate that the gardens, as the women remembered from their first visit, were laid out as they were during the eighteenth century—in short, the women concluded, during the days of Marie Antoinette. And the date, the tenth of August, coincided with the anniversary of the sacking of the Tuileries on August 10th, 1792.

From these points and many others, detailed in *An Adventure,* the authors concluded that they had, by some inexplicable twist of fate, walked that day into the memory of the unfortunate Queen, possibly on the theory that strong emotions linger in a particular place and that the psychically sensitive can be abnormally receptive to these emotions in such an atmosphere. By this line of reasoning, then, Miss Jourdain and Miss Moberly felt that the unhappiness and despair felt by the Queen at the sacking of the Tuileries mingled with her earlier pleasant, and rather wistful, memories of happier days spent at the Petit Trianon.

Did Anne Moberly and Eleanor Jourdain walk back into the past by some inexplicable psychical evasion of time? They thought they had when they presented their opinions of that afternoon in *An Adventure.* A book that took almost nine years to research and write can hardly be considered as a deliberate hoax; these women were scholars with academic reputations to protect. Even though the book was written under pseudonyms, they must have realized that the true authorship would be soon known. But their scholarship was more that of the academic historian rather than of the pure scientist.

Here lies the chief objection to the ladies' story. They waited until their experience could mellow and mature, like a fine wine, before beginning to study and evaluate the facts of the case. Several months passed before they put down on paper their independent accounts of the day at Versailles. This procedure is all very well for the historian; it is totally wrong for the scientific investigator, who must judge the nature of the event when it happens for a proper comparison with a similar experience.

What actually did the teachers see on that August afternoon? They concluded nine years later that they had seen ghosts, or apparitions, in a ghostly setting. Some authorities distinguish between the two by claiming a ghost is unknown to the percipient, while an apparition is known and frequently occurs as a result of the percipient's unconscious projections. In this case both definitions could apply. When first viewing the mysterious men and women at the Petit Trianon, the women took them for complete strangers, unknown to them. After nine years of study, however, they were able to decide that they had seen specific historical personalities, and identify each one seen during their walk.

They not only saw people but ghostly objects such as plows and spades, carts and bridges, cottages and the little bandstand. Surely spirits of the long dead do not usually return surrounded by the entire environment of their earthly life, as a sort of phantom stage set. It would be easy to object by saying that what the women saw on their walk was a complete illusion. But what powerful emotions did the two feel to create and project this joint illusion, complete down to the last detail of the shrubbery?

Were the ladies sharing a common hallucination? To do so would be to insist that they were both entranced at the time, a form of dual hypnosis. And how can the same hallucination or trance agree in so many details?

Here, of course, lies the unanswered question about

An Adventure and its authors. Because of their memories of the odd afternoon at the Petit Trianon, they felt compelled to follow nine years of research and study to explain their experience. The other side of the coin is, obviously, that their detailed memories of the day were almost wholly the result of their long research. It is difficult to disagree with the review of *An Adventure* in the "Proceedings of the Society for Psychical Research" in 1911, which said, "The foundations on which the supernormal claims of the *Adventure* are built are too slight, and too little allowance is made for weaknesses of human memory both in adding to and subtracting from facts—weaknesses from which there is no reason to think the writers of this book suffer less than the rest of the world."

CHAPTER NINE

The Psychic Life of Mrs. Tweedale

Who is a "sensitive" or a "psychic"? While the terms
may have several everyday meanings, to a psychical researcher they refer to a person who receives impressions
of his surroundings through means other than the usual
five senses. As the widely read author, Susy Smith, points
out, "It has been suggested that everyone is born with
ESP, but that in most people it is largely repressed in
favor of the more normal means of perception." The letters ESP stand for "extrasensory perception," the means
of gaining knowledge without the use of the five senses,
and without rational inference or guessing, Miss Smith
writes in her book, *ESP for the Millions.* This concept
of communication without normal sensory methods is not
an old wives' tale, nor should it be relegated to the realm
of myth or legend. Miss Smith tells us that this view is
considered most seriously by reputable and practical scientists; Sigmund Freud advanced the theory that forms of
ESP were the original means of human communication,
an idea also espoused by Duke University's Dr. Joseph
B. Rhine.

Yet most people consider such ideas as part and parcel of their childhood, to be brushed aside and ignored in the adult world. When a child everybody heard of some adult—an elderly aunt or an eccentric cousin, perhaps— who was said to have second sight, to experience premonitions, one who frequently had prophetic and ominous dreams which often came true. Perhaps they might themselves have had such experiences. Later, of course, the rational explanations for these events are found, and these stories are taken no more seriously than are ghosts, apparitions, and other unseen visitors.

There are some, however, who do not forget these ideas when they grow up, not because they possess a childlike personality, but because they may have undergone these experiences more often than the average person. So often, in fact, that they stop to wonder why. What is it about them that makes these unaccountable experiences happen so frequently? Why do their prophetic dreams seem to occur with such intensity? How is it that they, more than most people, are able to understand what others think without words? Their curiosity aroused, they consider the problem—and problem it certainly can be—with open, inquiring minds. And then the idea emerges: could it be that they are what is called a psychic or a sensitive?

One such person at the turn of the century was Violet Tweedale, the Scottish born novelist, political activist, crusader for women's rights, welfare worker, and friend and confidante of the rich and the powerful. She was also a psychic and a sensitive, she tells us, in her remarkable book, *Ghosts I Have Seen*, published in 1919. Mrs. Tweedale describes at length in her book the psychical experiences she enjoyed throughout her life, from her earliest childhood memories and spanning almost a half century. She tells of seeing ghosts and apparitions, of attending seances and the manifestations she saw at them, of seeing phantoms of the living and apparitions of the dead, of communicating with the spirits and forwarding messages at their request. She speaks of being able to discern a person's state of mind and mood from his aura, of committing and solving murders through psychic sensitivity, of sharing rooms with completely visible ghosts, and, on one occasion, of receiving a successful tip on the races from the spirit world. She spent, she says, forty years deep in occultism of all varieties. And enjoyed every minute of it.

Who was this unusual woman? Violet Tweedale was born in Edinburgh in 1862, the daughter of Robert Chambers who, with his father and uncle, published *Chambers Journal*. The family was wealthy and well-connected, and young Violet enjoyed all of the advantages of a well-born and rich Victorian childhood. *Chambers Journal* was among the leading literary magazines of the era and, as she describes it, as financially successful as it was intellectually stimulating. Her father followed the leisurely daily routine of a gentleman of affairs, spending a few hours at the office, dinner at four in the afternoon, then working on his articles on those evenings when he was not attending the theater or a social function.

Mr. Chambers had a good deal of time on his hands and spent much of it with his children, particularly Violet. This was for the best, she writes, since it helped to stimulate and broaden her mind which, following nineteenth century practice, was not exposed to formal education beyond the rudiments of reading, writing, arithmetic. Well respected in his community and in the literary world, Mr. Chambers was the model of a Victorian gentleman in all respects. He did, of course, have some eccentricities, among them a total disregard for money and the unusual habit of carrying packets of diamonds in his pockets to fondle and cheerfully display to his friends. Her father also had an abiding interest in the occult and the supernatural, and possibly from her association with him, Violet was predisposed to accept and understand the unknown.

Among her first memories, at the age of six, was lying in the nursery with her brother before drifting off to sleep and waiting with excited anticipation for what they called "Silk Dress" and "Rumpus." Every night the children would hear the tap of footsteps and the rustling of heavy silk skirts mounting the staircase, up two flights of stairs, and then down the corridor past their half-opened door, disappearing into the silence of a storage room at the end of the hallway. No person was ever seen, nor did the children ever hear the unseen walker go back downstairs. The mysterious sounds did not frighten the Chambers children, who spoke of them freely and looked forward to their return each night.

Nor were Violet and her brother frightened by "Rumpus" which came usually at five in the morning. They would awaken to an absolute pandemonium of noise in the nursery, as if the room was possessed by poltergeists throwing the furniture around wildly, banging and crashing against the walls, and shoving the bedsteads around. Then after a few moments the racket would stop and calm return to the nursery. Nothing was ever seen to move, though, and the family assumed that the children were having nightmares.

Violet's father died when she was in her twenties, and, left with a private income, she moved to London to live a more independent life. There she moved in older and more intellectual circles, counting among her friends the novelist, Mrs. Linton; a painter, Lord Leighton; and the great poet, Robert Browning. Violet considered Browning a highly developed mystic and spent many hours with him discussing the world of the spirit and its possible influence on his work. At that time Browning's poetry was considered difficult and obscure, because of the lack of proper sensitivity and spiritual perception on the part of the readers, in Mrs. Tweedale's opinion. She herself felt that Browning's works were quite probably influenced or directed from the spirit world.

Another valued friend during this period was Marie, Countess of Caithness and Duchess de Pomar, who Mrs. Tweedale considered a mystic of great advancement. Lady Caithness lived in Paris in a house called Holyrood and was devoted to the memory of Mary, Queen of Scots. Like many aristocratic Scots of the time. Lady Caithness was an ardent Jacobite and always dressed in the fashion of Mary Stuart, duplicating her costumes as closely as possible. While many said that Lady Caithness thought herself to be the reincarnation of the unhappy Stuart queen, Violet Tweedale disagrees. Holyrood House held a chapel or seance room dedicated to Queen Mary, the chief feature of which was a life-sized portrait of the dead monarch. Here Lady Caithness customarily held forth in conversation with the spirit of the Queen. It was this habit that gave rise to the unfounded rumors about Lady Caithness, according to Mrs. Tweedale.

Another fascinating encounter the young woman had with the spirit world was her meeting with Prince Valori at Nice. The Prince, long a topic of discussion in mystic circles, was always accompanied by his familiar, a man dressed in brown like a satyr at a masquerade. After seeing the figure with the Prince many times without being introduced, Mrs. Tweedale inquired from a Princess Schehoffskoi who the nobleman's companion was. A familiar, the Princess explained, acquired unwillingly at a Witch's Sabbath in the Vosges.

A turning point in Mrs. Tweedale's life was her meeting Helena Petrova Blavatsky, newly arrived in London to teach and expound her doctrines. While she found Madame Blavatsky a figure of commanding presence and power, it was the teacher's doctrines that attracted Mrs. Tweedale. She admits to abandoning orthodox religion at the age of twenty and seeking a greater fulfillment of her mystical needs. On hearing Madame Blavatsky expound her ideas, particularly the doctrines of reincarnation and karma, Mrs. Tweedale knew at once that she had found her answer in the religious and mystical sphere.

Mrs. Tweedale read Blavatsky's *The Secret Doctrine* through seven times in seven keys, as she puts it, and was thoroughly convinced of the truth it contained. Despite those who considered Madame Blavatsky a fraud and a charlatan, Mrs. Tweedale writes that she never wavered in her beliefs. The implications of fraud she ascribes to Madame Blavatsky's prankish nature and the fact that she was a thoroughly proficient conjurer, who had no desire to display true supernormal phenomena before the idle sensation seeker. To the initiate, however, it was a different matter; Mrs. Tweedale writes that she has on at least two occasions seen phantoms or astral projections in the Blavatsky salon, and that the teacher once gave her the ability to hear the ineffable music of life, an experience of which she had no doubt. She was not a good subject for hypnotism, she says.

Again, in her efforts to enlarge her mystic horizons, Mrs. Tweedale investigated spiritualism during the 1880's, patiently attending twenty-nine seances of all types until at last she finally witnessed a display of telekinesis, which proved to her the validity of the spiritualist hypotheses. She then discovered that she, too, was a medium, that is, sensitive to directions from the spirit world. With the assistance of her husband, she used the ouija board and took communications from a certain spirit for a number of years, passing on messages at the spirit's direction. Finally, much to her relief, Mrs. Tweedale's psychic capacity in this respect was exhausted, and the demanding spirit transferred his attentions to a different medium.

Unlike many writers of psychical phenomena, Mrs. Tweedale was not shy about using the term "ghosts" when referring to apparitions or phantoms of the dead. From early childhood she looked forward to the day when she would finally see a phantom, and was at last rewarded one November night when walking with her father. Their strolls often took them to a neighboring house that was reputedly haunted by a family ghost, although the elderly sisters in the house never mentioned the subject. The house stood on extensive grounds which were surrounded by high walls and tall, old trees. This dark and stormy night as Violet and her father were walking up the drive toward the dark house, they saw a figure appear at the corner of the building toward them. The figure was of a woman wearing a white nightgown and her long, black hair was streaming behind her with the wind. They stood dumfounded as the distraught woman ran through the grounds down the drive toward the gate. Then, as she passed them, Mr. Chambers set off in pursuit of the phantom, only to return to his disappointed daughter in a few moments. "Vanished into thin air," he told Violet with chagrin, "just as I reached her. That's always the way. You can't catch them."

Another visit for tea at a different house resulted in seeing a second ghost. Here the father and daughter called on an old lady, who lived in a big house with only one servant, surrounded by the past and her memories. They were served tea in the drawing room, which opened onto the garden. Violet looked up during the conversation to see the figure of a middle-aged, gray-haired woman wandering aimlessly through the flower beds. The woman appeared as if she was dazed and confused, waving her hands about without purpose. She called the attention of her hostess to the figure, and the old lady fell to her knees and covered her face with the tea cloth to shut out the sight in the garden. The apparition lasted only for about four minutes, after which the visitors helped their hostess to her chair, and the conversation resumed politely with no mention of the woman in the garden. Later Mr. Chambers explained that the specter was that of the old lady's daughter, who had lived in the house for years, totally insane.

Once, while spending a summer with her husband in a cottage on the Thames, Mrs. Tweedale met an alcoholic ghost. The house faced the river with French doors opening onto the green lawn. In the dining room Mrs. Tweedale had furnished a sideboard as a bar for the refreshment of guests who had been out boating. While generally enjoying the weeks spent in the riverside cottage, Mrs. Tweedale always felt uneasy in the dining room, particularly whenever she was near the sideboard. Her sense of disquiet began when she put the sherry and the tantalus of whiskey on the sideboard. Whenever she was in the room, she felt her attention being drawn toward this bar. At first she could not understand what focused her psychic attention to this particular corner of the room, but then she began to see a gray cloud hovering over the sideboard. She realized at this time what was calling her to the spot; she was being asked to have a drink. Gradually this gray mist grew and took form, and its occult invitations became more insistent. The shadowy cloud took the shape of a small, attractive woman who hovered near the tantalus of whiskey, as if offering a drink and seeking company in the liquor. Upon investigation Mrs. Tweedale discovered the wraith's identity, and realized that she had once seen her when the woman had lived. The ghost was that of a demi-mondaine who had once lived in the cottage, and who had later died of acute alcoholism. While Mrs. Tweedale's sympathies went out to the unhappy shade, she resisted the occult invitations strenuously. She had for years been a total abstainer, she stated, believing firmly that a genuine medium must avoid liquor at all times.

Mrs. Tweedale's ghostly visitors were not only human spirits. Quite distressed by the death of her pet bulldog, Pompey, she found comfort in its return to the house and her company. Often she was able to hear his snuffling and the clatter of his phantom paws on the floor, and twice saw the bowlegged figure of the animal happily waddling down the drive before her. She strongly believes that animals have souls, too; to deny this fact would be to deny all ideals of immortality, she writes.

While seldom frightened by the sight of a specter—genuine mediums rarely are, she indicates—Mrs. Tweedale in 1900 experienced her first fear when confronted by a silent visitation. The ghost appeared to her in the bedroom of her London house; she awoke one night and saw a man sitting in her armchair by the fire, holding a piece of paper loosely in his hand. The figure did not speak to her or even attempt to look at her, but simply sat staring into the fire. Yet she was seized by absolute, paralyzing panic and in terror pulled the bedclothes over her face to shut out the sight of the ghost. The next day she attempted to sort out her thoughts and rationalize her terror. She had been confronted by ghosts before and knew that she needn't be afraid in their presence, since they had the right to share a house with the living. Yet, when the apparition occurred again, she felt the same wave of horror sweep over her.

The figure in her fireside chair was that of a young man of about thirty, clean-shaven and wearing a powdered wig, dressed in blue coat and breeches in the style of a naval officer of the time of Lord Nelson. She always saw the man in profile and at no time did he ever notice her presence in the room, but sat with his head bowed in thought staring into the fire. The ghost came at frequent intervals to Mrs. Tweedale and, while she overcame her original panic at his presence, her nerves were completely on edge with the unwanted presence. Finally, on the advice of an understanding friend, she sought the assistance of a Franciscan monk who was known to be an exorcist, and with his spiritual aid, set the phantom free from his earthly subjection.

A skeptic could point out that Mrs. Tweedale's ghostly visitors always came just as she was falling asleep or waking, and that she might well have been dreaming. But it was not only in these drowsy moments that she saw ghosts and disembodied spirits, she tells us. On a cold October morning while walking through the park of a great estate toward the house she noticed a young woman walking some thirty feet ahead of her. Mrs. Tweedale was feeling the bite of the autumn wind though properly dressed against the cold, yet she was astonished to see that the woman before her was wearing only a thin muslin dress. She did not see the woman's face under the large, concealing bonnet, so she could not recognize the person. She walked faster to catch up with the scantily dressed woman and introduce herself, but the woman walked just as quickly toward the mansion. Then Mrs. Tweedale noticed a friend coming down from the house toward her, and thought that this friend might recognize the lady in the bonnet. Suddenly when the muslin gowned figure was equally distant from Mrs. Tweedale and her friend, it vanished instantly. The friend was unable to identify the figure, it seemed, since there was no face beneath the old-fashioned bonnet. Spirits of this nature, solid and lifelike, are always with us, the author says, and we often see them on the streets and stand next to them in crowds without realizing that these figures are disembodied phantoms, no longer living.

The subject of auras always fascinated Violet Tweedale, since she claimed to have been born with the ability to see them, and was not aware until an adult that most people did not have this power. An aura, in her terms, is nothing more than a halo, and every living person possesses one, the astral counterpart of his human atmosphere. And while it is not clear whether an aura is a projection of a person's spiritual development or a magnetic emanation of his physical makeup, still science has been able to photograph them and thus prove their existence.

While habituated to seeing auras, Mrs. Tweedale does not consider them easy to describe, any more than the human face. As the face changes its expression to reflect emotions, so does an aura change in color, shape, and character. Because of this, incidents and people can be fixed positively in memory. Prime Minister Gladstone she remembers because of his three foot aura, which was largely purple, the color of power. She also remembers passing a little glove shop in France and from the outside seeing the brilliant fury of an enormous golden aura, which proved to belong to the Empress Elizabeth of Austria, later assassinated. Not that auras are solely one color; they are, instead, prismatic in tone, with one color of the spectrum predominating. Mr. Frederic W. H. Myers' aura displayed the entire rainbow, however, and was unusually composed of an aura within an aura, one surrounding the other. These are the auras of the great and the spiritually advanced, though; the average person's aura will hardly be so outstanding in color or size.

Certain colors signify definite emotional states to Mrs. Tweedale. Crimson shows anger, of course—a person is "seeing red"—while rose is the color of love. Green indicates jealousy, yellow means envy, and gray indicates a disgruntled, gloomy person. The dull orange auras belong to extreme materialists, while the high intellectuals and spiritually joyful people are marked by auras of brilliant golden yellow. An off-color blue shows a depressed person, but an aura of clear sky blue surrounds the artist and the pure scientist. The powerful and the mighty carry auras of royal purple and, delightfully, all children until the age of seven have auras of crystal purity. The spiritually or morally tarnished will display a small and tattered aura; shapes vary in an almost infinite number. Perhaps the most unusual aura Mrs. Tweedale saw belonged to a friend she does not identify. Nor does she explain the significance of her friend's aura; it was lopsided.

During her travels Mrs. Tweedale had many encounters with elementals. These have been defined as natural spirits of low intelligence deriving their power from the traditional four elements of nature, earth, air, fire, and water. Some authorities also state that elementals are discarnate subhuman spirits, possessing at best an extremely primitive intelligence, a description that could easily describe the poltergeist.

Mrs. Tweedale herself thinks that elementals can be divided into two classes: nature spirits formed out of the elemental essence of the mineral kingdom, and artificial elementals called into being by conscious or unconscious human thought or will. Artificial elementals can be willed into existence by magicians, often to serve malignant purposes, and are the familiars of witches and practitioners of black magic. The same artificial elementals can be brought into being by simple curiosity, however, since their essence is extraordinarily sensitive to human thought.

They usually reflect the character of the person who thought them into existence, although this character is often wildly distorted.

Once when Mrs. Tweedale was visiting friends she encountered such prankish, artificial elementals. The previous owner of the house had when living been unhealthily interested in witchcraft and black magic, despite Mrs. Tweedale's warnings that she was tampering with little understood and frequently dangerous powers, thus acquiring unhealthy tastes that might carry over to the astral plane and be difficult to discontinue.

The amateur witch in life was aware of Mrs. Tweedale's one abhorrence, that of the large, furry moths that appear in the early summer, fluttering around lights, dropping and blundering into people without warning. While able to face almost anything of this world or the other, Mrs. Tweedale could not stand the sight or sound of these moths, which she found repulsive, sinister, and uncanny.

When visiting, Mrs. Tweedale was given this dead witch's bedroom for her use. Dressing for dinner she could feel nothing wrong with the atmosphere; if she had, she could have asked for a different room, since her present hostess was also an understanding psychic. As she changed, however, she began to hear strange rustling sounds in the shadowy twilight. Then suddenly two of the distasteful moths fell out of nowhere onto the bed. Shrinking in disgust, she called the maid to remove the creatures. The moths, she realized, could have flown in through the window, in spite of the maid's claim to have kept the windows closed. She did not mention the matter to her hostess during dinner. When she came into the bedroom that night, to her horror she discovered the bed covered with moths, even though the windows were closed. Choking back her nausea she counted almost thirty of the largest moths she had ever seen, easily three inches in length. She realized that she couldn't sleep in that room, so she spent the night quietly and without disturbance in a spare bedroom.

At dinner the next night she told her hostess of the experience and, when the woman showed a certain skepticism, took her to the bedroom. Again the bed was barely visible under a blanket of squirming, fluttering gray moths. It was obvious to both women that Mrs. Tweedale was the object of an occult practical joke played by the dead witch.

A more cheerful encounter with elementals occurred in an inn while Mrs. Tweedale was traveling in Bohemia. In the middle of the night she was awakened by high-pitched shouts of happiness and saw, in the moonlight, a dozen non-human creatures playing leapfrog around the room. Amazed, she watched the small pseudo-men cavorting, their three-foot human bodies surmounted by the heads of apes. She then turned on the light for a better view and the creatures continued their gleeful game, but gradually faded out of existence, as if the light sapped and drained them of their power.

Among the characteristics of a psychic is the ability to sense a disturbed atmosphere and discern a haunted room. A room in which great emotional and mental turmoil has taken place seems to harbor these emotions long afterward. Hate, terror, sorrow, all the intense emotions linger and impress themselves on the person who, either by nature or training, has the increased sensitivity to gather these impressions.

For Mrs. Tweedale a haunted room is quickly discerned, even in bright daylight, since it is full of shadows. These shadows seem to originate in the corners of the room, stretching over the floor, hovering and vibrating, dissipating and reforming, like gray drifts of smoke. Such rooms invariably hold an oppressive shadow over a person's head, floating motionlessly between the floor and ceiling.

The impressions gathered by a psychic person in a haunted room can be overpowering sometimes. In the tower room of a Scottish castle she was visiting, Mrs. Tweedale felt the shadows closing in rapidly and with great malignancy. She intuitively knew that the room was haunted by a spirit of distinct evil, and felt unseen eyes watching every move she made. The center of the horror to her was a mirror over a chest of drawers. She quickly covered this mirror with a towel, but still felt the evil emanations from the glass. She was drawn toward this mirror even though she knew that she must not under any circumstances uncover and look into the glass. Finally at the breaking point, she made the sign of the cross in an attempt to exorcize the evil, but with only temporary results. Whatever had been there would return later that night, so in spite of insulting her hosts who had put her into the tower room, she invented an excuse and fled the castle as quickly as possible.

A similar experience happened when she stayed for a night at a country inn in Scotland. She had a horrifying and vivid dream in which she felt that she had committed murder in a London house and returned to the scene of her crime at night to hide the corpse in a more secret place. While attempting to do so, she was discovered by a gentleman entering the front hallway and escaped by feigning sonambulism. While the dream was frighteningly clear in detail up to this point, the horrible climax was shrouded in cloud, and then she woke. This nightmare recurred over a period of thirty years, long after she left the inn and inspired both terror and revulsion in her. Mrs. Tweedale never discovered who had occupied the room at the inn before she did, but was convinced that the actual killer had slept there, probably just after the murder. She says that just as a physical illness can be caught from sleeping in an infected bed, so can a mental illness, since the emotions, and especially fear, are highly contagious.

But if the baser emotions are contagious, so are the finer to the psychic. This she realized when visiting Lourdes, the great shrine and center of prayer in France. Calling Lourdes the "concentrated essence of prayer," Mrs. Tweedale writes that the psychic cannot help but be caught up in its atmosphere. It was here while looking out over a square thronged with supplicants that she saw in the sky the figure of an angel. The vision lasted for three minutes, and the author describes with great power the huge, brooding figure hovering over the crowd, wingless and wrapped in a cloud of gray. Here, too, she experienced another vision. While receiving the Eucharist according to Anglican rites she saw the chalice disappear and be replaced by what she calls the "Flaming Heart," at which point she claims to have intuitively and ecstatically understood the divine mysteries of the spirit.

Was Mrs. Tweedale an authentic medium and psychic? In *Ghosts I Have Seen* she has described a lifetime of psychic experiences, but without documentation to support her claims or any details of experimental techniques she may have used to verify the phenomena she has heard and seen. She tells of her experiences, however, with the controlled discipline and style of a literate and professional author, not as a sensation-seeking matron with too much time on her hands. It is said that she attended seances in the company of Lord Balfour, Lord Haldane, and W. E. Gladstone, hardly the sort of men who would waste their time with a foolish, gullible woman.

Many of her accounts bear the marks of truth and have much in common with similar cases seriously investigated by the Society for Psychical Research. Her descriptions of astral phenomena, her encounters with disembodied spirits in the presence of others, her sensitivity to occult atmosphere and emotions, even her perception of auras; these, had they been properly studied, might well have had a basis in fact. Clairvoyance, telekinesis, telepathy—extrasensory perception, in other words—can no longer be called a parlor game. It is a serious field of endeavor for many reputable scientists today.

A case in point is Mrs. Tweedale's winning tip on the races. While getting into her carriage after a visit with a psychic friend, she suddenly remembered her husband's joking request to ask for the name of a winner at a Newmarket meet. The answer came as she drove off, advising which horse would win and which would place. The Tweedales backed both horses at long odds, and were delighted when they won. But in thanking her friend for the tip, Mrs. Tweedale was told that there had been no answer, in fact that her friend took no interest in racing and knew nothing of the subject. Mrs. Tweedale wondered, then, if because her mind was open for an answer, possibly a spirit of a horse-fancier may have given her the tip. Perhaps; there may also have been a knowledgable racing fan in the party however who mentally had answered Mrs. Tweedale's question. Today's explanation could well be ESP.

CHAPTER TEN

Exorcising Demons
and Expelling Ghosts

What does a person do if his house is haunted by an earthbound spirit? There are a multitude of stories telling of unhappy ghosts lingering at the scene of their earthly lives, often with a definite purpose to their appearances, such as righting a wrong, seeking justice for their memory, or asking for a proper burial. Then, too, there are accounts of houses being haunted by definitely malevolent and evil spirits, who seem to direct their spectral malice toward the living. While many owners of the fabled great mansions of England and Scotland seem to take great pride in their ghosts who walk the long halls, others feel distinctly uncomfortable in sharing their homes with the unexpected visitors from the spirit world, and cast about in a certain desperation for the methods of ridding their houses of the uninvited phantoms. When troubled by a bothersome specter, people often find the breaking of the ghostly lease even more difficult than removing an unpleasant human tenant.

The Jesuit writer, Father Herbert Thurston, points out in his book, *Ghosts and Poltergeists,* that neither the medieval nor the modern service books of his church take much notice of hauntings and earthbound spirits. He says that the *Rituale Romanum,* the books giving the required Catholic ceremonials and prayers, seems to ignore the possibility of ghosts of the dead returning to their earthly surroundings. Though his church provides solemn ceremonies for expelling evil spirits from possessing the living, it does not recognize the necessity of banishing a malign spirit from a house.

The Catholic Church has always recognized that a person could be possessed by an evil spirit, basing its view on Scriptural references to cases of possession by the devil. In fact, such human possession is thought of as being diabolic in origin, and must in Roman practice be treated with extreme care and seriousness. Among the Church's Articles of Canon Law, the *Codex juris ecclesiastici,* governing the conduct of the church, are Articles 1151, 1152, and 1153 concerning the proper conduct of a solemn ceremony of exorcism to free a person from diabolic possession. First, of course, the existence of such possession must be established, and the priest must consider the case as carefully as a physician making a correct and sound medical diagnosis. The evidence required as proof of truly diabolic possession consists essentially of four elements: the presence of an obviously alien intelligence; the speaking or understanding by the possessed of an unknown language; his revealing secret or distant facts and events; and, finally, his displaying a superhuman physical strength.

Once the possession is established, the remedy is given through the rites of exorcism. An exorcism in such a case is an extraordinarily impressive ceremony, and is not to

127

be given at will or taken lightly by the priests; it is a ceremony conducted only by those specially designated by the Church. Part of the reason for the solemn consideration given to diabolic possession is the danger to the priestly exorcist in the presence of what he believes to be the devil. And most important is the danger to the condition of the possessed person himself. Another Catholic writer says that if true possession is not clearly established, the solemnity of the rites can endanger the sick person by conjuring up in his disturbed mind the picture of the devil, or of what the possessed person thinks is the devil.

The ceremonies of exorcism are lengthy, beginning with the sign of the Cross, a versicle, a prayer, and then the adjuration to the devil. Father Thurston quotes from an exorcism outlined in a seventeenth century Spanish manual, the conjuration stating in part, "I adjure thee, O serpent of old, by the Judge of the living and the dead, by the Creator of the world who hath power to cast into hell, that thou depart forthwith from this house . . . Hearken, then Satan, and fear . . ." This exorcism in Father Thurston's opinion is the only one he has found that might apply to a ghost-haunted house or place.

He does state, however, that many other church ceremonies frequently begin with minor forms of exorcism, among them the consecration of a church, the reconciliation of a desecrated sanctuary, and the solemn blessing of a cemetery. The sacraments of Baptism and Extreme Unction—the blessing of the dying—contain forms of exorcism, both designed to place the individual beyond the influence of evil. But for a place, apart from the old

Spanish ritual, he feels that the simple house blessings were intended to cover almost all situations.

Protestant churches, particularly during the sixteenth and seventeenth centuries when Europe was swept by beliefs in ghosts and witches, did not generally consider that alleged apparitions were the returned spirits of the long dead. Taking a sober view, most Protestant churches considered these spectral apparitions to be diabolic in origin and treated such cases with as solemn prayer as the Catholic Church, but without the lengthy formal rituals. Direct action was frequently called for, and the ink-stained wall where Martin Luther threw the inkwell at the demon which was bedevilling him can be seen today. The Reverend Samuel Wesley, father of Methodism's founder, shook his fist at the invisible spirit plaguing his young children and, calling him "Thou deaf and dumb devil," commanded that the spirit follow him to his study where he could be dealt with by a man.

Today little notice is given by the various churches to the problems of expelling the bothering spirit from houses that are supposed to be haunted. However, the use of a psychic medium as the instrument for this purpose has become more common, with varying degrees of success. In *Unbidden Guests,* William Oliver Stevens tells of a case in which attempts were made to rid a house of its ghosts by the famous medium, Eileen Garrett, with Dr. Nandor Fodor taking command of the affair.

The haunting occurred at a country manor house in England during the mid-1930's. Although the house was known to be haunted, the new owners had not been told this when they bought the house and moved there with their daughter. The couple were themselves unhappy and completely dissolute, the wife being a drug addict and the husband an alcoholic. It is the couple's emotional conflicts that provided the foundations for the ghost's appearances, in the opinions of those who studied the affair.

The ghost made his appearance by knocking loudly on the husband's bedroom door late one night, the sounds being also heard by the wife in her own room. The knocking continued for two more nights. Then on the fourth visit, the husband was awake and heard the same loud rapping. He looked up and saw a strangely dressed figure of sinister appearance standing in his doorway. The figure was of an old man dressed in a dirty tunic and leggings, a soft hat, and a kerchief at the neck. On being asked to explain his presence, the old man said nothing but continued to stare at the householder. The husband then became furious and rushed at the figure to throw him out, but his hands went through the old man's body. In terror, the husband ran to his wife's room and fainted. His wife was completely alarmed and ran out into the hall to look for brandy to revive her husband. There she, too, saw the same malignant figure, so solid in appearance that she thought he was living. She also demanded an explanation and, receiving no answer, struck at the old man. Like her husband, her hands went through the apparition and struck the door painfully. At this point the couple realized that the hideous visitor was a phantom.

The ghostly visitations occurred almost two dozen times, accompanied by loud knocks and the heavy sound of footsteps. On one occasion the ghost showed his throat to the couple and they saw that it had been cut from ear to ear. As the ghastly visits continued the couple grew panicky and attempted a religious exorcism, but with no success. It was at this point that they sought the help of Dr. Fodor, long a leader in the field of psychical research. Dr. Fodor in turn sought out the help of Mrs. Garrett, knowing that she had been successful in several cases in eliminating spirit disturbances from certain houses. He told Mrs. Garrett only that the house in question was haunted, but did not describe the nature of the incidents or tell her anything of the unhappy couple.

On the first visit, the group met in the husband's bedroom. Mrs. Garrett soon went into a trance and her control, Uvani, appeared speaking through her. Dr. Fodor then spoke to the spirit control, asking for his help for both the unhappy ghost and the beleagured householders. The control answered at length by describing the unpleasant emotional tensions existing in the house between the couple, and stated that this atmosphere provided the environment for the ghost to return. The control, Uvani, then said that the restless spirit was out of time and did not know that he was dead. To rid the house of the ghost, the control said that he must stand aside and let the ghost take possession of the medium. He could then be communicated with and thus be made to understand his situation; with this would come his release.

Shortly afterward the nature of Mrs. Garrett's trance changed. While relaxed when under the control of Uvani, she now grew rigid and then began fumbling at her throat and tongue, muttering and groaning as she did so. She then fell to her knees and remained in this position for some time before she began to speak, this time in a different man's voice. From the long conversation that followed, the members of the group were able to discover the nature of the ghost and the reason for his hauntings. He was the spirit of a sixteenth century landholder who had been betrayed by his lord, who then seduced the landholder's wife and made off with his son, and left the landholder to die in a long forgotten dungeon prison. He came, he said, to seek vengeance on his lord, and to find his wife and son. Finally made to understand that he was dead, he became rather pathetic in manner and pleaded to be restored to his wife and son. This the group promised to accomplish at the next meeting.

The party felt then that they had successfully laid the ghost, but the couple were not convinced and said that the spirit might return. And he did, a day later, terrifying the husband and wife again. They reached Dr. Fodor then, who arranged for further seances to resolve the matter. The last with Mrs. Garrett as the medium took place in London. As before, her control first appeared and then the ghost took control. He spoke as unhappily as before, and the group continued to explain his situation to him. At last he understood clearly and agreed to his dismissal, saying that he went in peace.

Violet Tweedale tells in her book of a similar experience in releasing a ghost from a haunted house. This ghost was not visible, yet manifested itself in three different types of phenomena. Piercing shrieks and screams were heard to come from the house at all hours of the day and night, screams that could not be traced to peacocks on the neighboring estate. In the house, called Castel A Mare, the doors were constantly being locked or unlocked by unseen hands, and then the sound of invisible feet could be heard running through the corridors and up and down the staircase.

The haunted house stood by the sea in the resort town of Torquay, backing onto the road and facing the ocean, with a long balcony on the second floor. The three-story building had long been known as haunted in the neighborhood, and for some years had stood vacant, since few tenants would remain there very long. The gardens and the stables were also considered haunted, but most of the disturbances centered about the house itself, particularly in two rooms on the second floor. Mrs. Tweedale and her husband had heard of the house's reputation for some time, and were eager to investigate the rumors and "take the atmosphere" to see if the stories had any basis in fact. They asked the owner for the keys, explaining their purpose, and permission to investigate was readily given.

The couple decided to do their ghost hunting during the day, between one and two o'clock in the afternoon when most of the townspeople would be at dinner and would not bother them. On entering the building the Tweedales immediately sensed the disturbed atmosphere of the house and found that the most unhealthy rooms were a small room on the second floor and its adjoining bathroom, which had once been a closet. While roaming the deserted house, they, too, heard the frightening screams and the sounds of the running feet. They searched but saw no intruders, nor any signs of them; all of the windows were dusty and clouded with cobwebs, which eliminated the chance that any person had entered in that fashion. They had locked the front door behind them and found no indications that it had been forced. After their first visit, they closed all of the doors inside and placed a heap of brush and twigs by the front door when leaving the house.

On the following day they were gratified to find that the pile of twigs was still undisturbed. Yet, once inside the house, to their surprise they found all of the doors open even though they had left them closed the day before. Other phenomena which happened this day were the sight of a door knob being turned by unseen hands and again the running footsteps. They followed the same procedure when leaving and on the third visit found the doors again open. Then, while coming down the staircase they heard the sounds of somebody brushing against the wall near them, as if trying to escape detection. Again the couple saw nothing. This day before leaving the house, the Tweedales locked the bathroom door and carefully hid the key in the house in a place where no trespasser could possibly find it. Yet, returning the next day, they saw the bathroom door unlocked and open, even though the hidden key had not been disturbed.

Before leaving Torquay the Tweedales talked with a former tenant of the house, one who had lived there some thirty years earlier. This tenant confirmed the house's haunted reputation and verified all of the phenomena, saying that the drawing room had been uninhabitable because of a crowd of invisible people moving and walking about.

Later in 1917 Mrs. Tweedale was invited to return to Castel A Mare as part of a group interested in studying the mysterious house further. The party consisted of Mrs. Tweedale, four other women, a soldier on leave from his regiment, a neighboring businessman, and a professional medium, described as being tiny and frail. Again the visit was made during the day, and they assembled in the second-floor bedroom, standing by the walls while the medium sat on a crate. The medium went slowly into a trance, which deepened, until in about ten minutes she was seized by a violent masculine personality. The spirit began to shout and swear abusively at the party, asking why they intruded into his house and threatened his privacy. Shaking the medium's fists, the spirit ordered them from the house and offered to throw them out if they refused. The party shrank away from the medium toward the bathroom-closet, and this seemed to throw the spirit into a frenzy. The medium suddenly flew at the soldier and clawed and struck at the man until she drew blood. Mrs. Tweedale says that she and the businessman tried to help the soldier, while the other women ran from the house in terror. They found the medium possessed of incredible strength as she fought them off and away from the bathroom. She finally forced them out of the bedroom and onto the landing, at which point the spirit left and the medium collapsed. The men carried the unconscious woman out into the garden where the group worked diligently for ten minutes until she revived.

Several days after this visit to the haunted house, a smaller group returned with the medium; three of the women from the first party refused to come back. As before, the medium became entranced in the bedroom and was quickly and violently possessed by the furious male spirit, who again attempted to force them away from the bathroom. This time, however, the party fought the possessing spirit and the soldier continued to repeat a form of exorcism. The group succeeded in forcing the medium against the bedroom wall, where she collapsed in a heap on the floor as the man's spirit left her. As the group looked on in wonder, they saw a second spirit take control of the medium, crouched on the floor. This spirit was a woman or girl and caused the medium to moan and sob in terror; then the woman pointed toward the side of the room and pleaded with them to help her master. This spirit was evidently once that of a servant in the house, and the clutching at her throat in anguish seemed to indicate to the group that somehow death by strangulation had taken place in the bedroom.

Then all at once the same piercing screams of horror were heard, coming from the throat of the medium, as she turned and began to fight for her life against an invisible assailant. The woman shrieked for help against the unseen man who was trying to kill her, and while the soldier continued his attempts to exorcise the first spirit, Mrs. Tweedale joined in the battle. The soldier's efforts were finally successful in routing the vicious male ghost, and a rather battered and dishevelled party listened as the ghost gave them more details of the long-forgotten tragedy. The violent male spirit was that of a foreign-born doctor who had killed his mentally deficient patient before the horrified eyes of the servant, then killed her too. The corpses were hidden in the closet, which later became the bathroom, and accounted for the violent efforts to prevent any of the party from going into that room. The spirit gave the group the name of the dead master, and the date of the crime, but Mrs. Tweedale does not say in her narrative whether any of the party verified these facts. Finally exhausted by her story, the spirit left the medium, who collapsed in the fatal room and was carried outside and revived. Mrs. Tweedale remarks on the fact that this tiny, fragile psychic when revived showed no signs of physical or mental exhaustion, or any knowledge of her activities when entranced.

Whether this experiment succeeded in banishing the formidable ghost from Castel A Mare, the author does not say. However, she states that on a winter night some months later she passed the house on the road, and again heard the sound of running footsteps and torrents of derisive laughter from the darkened windows.

These, then, are some of the methods and procedures that have been used to lay a ghost and cleanse the premises of malign influences. Are they successful? The psychical researcher would feel that the use of a sensitive or medium could lay bare the emotional and psychological elements that form the foundation for a haunting of this nature, and thus convince the spirit to depart. The clergyman might disagree, though, and prefer the more orthodox and traditional means in banishing a spirit. Perhaps the best answer lies in the psyche of the person being haunted.

CHAPTER ELEVEN

The Haunted Realists

Are you superstitious? Do you avoid black cats and walking under ladders? Or do you throw salt over your left shoulder after spilling some at the table?

And what of spirits or ghosts? Do you believe in them? On dark, moonless nights do you avoid passing a cemetery? Do you make certain that the hallways are well-lighted if you are alone at home on certain nights?

Today ninety-nine of a hundred adults would laugh in your face if you asked such questions. Friends would scoff if you admitted such beliefs and would label these notions as ignorance and base superstition. Our common sense shows that ideas of this nature are false and illogical, ideas that should be relegated to an earlier and less enlightened age.

After all, this is the age of science and of common sense, when we know better than to believe in credulous superstitious carryovers such as phantoms or spirit materializations. Ours is the scientific generation where, by drawing on the breathtakingly rapid advances in human knowledge, man can scientifically determine the cause-

and-effect relationship of nature and his environment. He can comprehend and measure both qualitatively and quantitatively his world and universe.

In short, ours is the Generation of Realists.

It is today's realists who assume that man has reached the outermost borders of his knowledge and who will not accept any form of natural or supernatural phenomena which man's intellect cannot grasp or man's scientific methodology measure and classify.

Then what do such pragmatic realists do when faced with those phenomena for which their intellectual training has not prepared them?

Two such realists are Claire McCarthy and Stuart Chisholm of San Francisco, both of whom were separately confronted by the unexpected and the unknown recently. Although close friends for years, neither Miss McCarthy nor Mr. Chisholm was aware that the other was undergoing a similar encounter.

At a cocktail party a few weeks ago the conversation turned to those borderline areas of knowledge which have been so little explored, among which was psychical research and the supernormal. While most of the guests admitted little or no familiarity with these fields of investigation and scoffed with complete skepticism, the two friends hesitated slightly from wholeheartedly joining the general laughter. Finally Miss McCarthy told the group that, while she once had shared their opinions toward the supernatural and psychical research, she was no longer quite so certain that the subject was completely fraudulent.

She had been recently troubled, she said, by peculiar and curious incidents in her house that no amount of investigation or rationalization could explain. "You can laugh if you want," she said, "but finally I thought that my flat must be haunted."

Most of the guests were good friends of Claire's and knew her as a thoroughly practical and realistic woman. Her statement was greeted not with derision but with puzzled amazement. Stuart Chisholm looked at her seriously.

"You too?" he said.

The two have been friends for more than fifteen years, so close that most of their acquaintances considered them blood relatives. They were not mocked as if they were foolish and gullible people suffering from superheated imaginations. Their friends asked about the experiences and hauntings they claimed to have undergone, and while each only skimmed the surface of his own situation, it was clear that neither was joking about the matter. Briefly they traded accounts of the strange events that happened to them; then the conversation turned to different topics.

In talks with Miss McCarthy and Mr. Chisholm later, they expanded their stories of the unusual and extraordinary experiences they had separately undergone in their own apartments. Although they meet about once a week and telephone each other frequently, both claim that they knew nothing of each other's strange encounters until the cocktail party, nor had either discussed the matter with mutual acquaintances during the periods of the manifestations. Their individual stories are interesting because of their different reactions to the disturbances, as well as the varying nature of the phenomena themselves.

Miss McCarthy told the story of her experiences in her flat, which was the scene of the curious events she describes. A tall, thirty-five-year-old brunette, she worked as a private secretary until her retirement because of failing vision. In December, 1962, when she became aware of the inevitable deterioration of her sight, she bought a house in a quiet and secluded cul-de-sac high on San Francisco's famous Telegraph Hill. This house is a forty-year-old duplex and, until its renovation by the previous owner, was notorious as the neighborhood eyesore. The former owner completely renovated the building, however, making the necessary repairs to the structure, enclosing the tiny garden with a high brick wall, and completely rewiring the electrical system to bring the house up to the city's electrical code. After owning the house for some eighteen months, he then sold it to Miss McCarthy.

Claire McCarthy, a Liberal Arts alumnus of the Berkeley campus of the University of California, is a highly articulate woman and appears eminently practical and down to earth in her manner. Her acceptance and adjustment to oncoming blindness has been so skillfully accomplished that at first meeting a person would not realize that there was anything defective about her vision. She wears contact lenses to preserve the remains of her sight and does not give the slightest indication that her vision is less than twenty-twenty. Yet in her own opinion her failing eyesight at first obscured what she feels is the actual explanation for the abnormal incidents in her flat.

Miss McCarthy bought the old house for several reasons, the most important of which was her awareness of her eventual blindness and the necessity for a private and quiet place to live. She lives in the upper flat and rents the lower. Her flat is sunny and cheerful and is particularly suited by its arrangements to the needs of a person with limited sight.

The flat is reached by an outer staircase which ends on an outside porch running the full width of the flat. To the left of the entrance is a floor-to-ceiling double sliding glass door leading to the main room of the flat. There is a handle on the sliding glass door, but no outside latch or lock. These glass doors were installed at the time of the house's renovation, and are solid within their aluminum frames, with no loose fittings or gaps that could result from the shifting of such an old building on its foundations. From the porch, then, the only entrance to the flat is through the solid front door if the glass doors are locked from within. There is a back door on the street level at the bottom of an inner staircase, but for safety's sake this door is always kept locked and bolted from within.

But listen to Claire McCarthy's own story:

"I bought this house in December, 1962, after living in a flat in North Beach for several years. I hadn't been too satisfied in the old flat for some time; for one thing, the neighborhood was too noisy, even at night. By then I knew that I was going blind and that, even if the operations to save a little vision were successful, I would need all the privacy and peace I could find in the future.

"This house seemed ideal when it came up on the market. The two flats were in excellent condition, and the fact that the house and garden were screened from the street by the brick wall made for the best privacy a person could find these days in San Francisco. Well, after the usual drawn-out business arrangements, I bought the house and moved in just before Christmas. I put the lower flat up for lease then, but it wasn't taken for almost seven months so, you see, my tenant could have had nothing to do with what happened here."

"So, the first odd thing I noticed were the lights. No, it wasn't the lights; I take that back. Frankly, the first odd thing was the cat. At the time I didn't think so, but considering the whole affair, I feel now that the strange cat was the first unusual encounter.

"Let me say that I have never been afraid of cats. I've never had a cat or a dog, but I've never been afraid of them. No strong feelings about them at all; I suppose you could say that I'm indifferent to them.

"But it was that cat, the huge gray tomcat that was my first uncomfortable experience around here. I'd been living in the house for about three days when he first came around—'appeared' would be a better word, actually. This day I parked on the street—I could still drive then—and when I got out of the car, there was this gray cat sitting directly in front of the gate. Now, I hadn't seen him when I drove up, but with poor sight this could be expected. Well, he didn't move when I came to the gate, but just sat there absolutely still as if he were challenging me to go into my own house. I was surprised, to say the least, but then I shooed him away and went in. Or I thought I had chased him away. He must have jumped onto the wall and then into the garden, because when I started toward the stairs there he was again, sitting and staring. How he did it I don't understand—the wall is about eight feet high. Again I said 'scat', and he trotted up the stairs right in front of me. When I got to the top on the porch, there he was again sitting on the porch railing. And staring at me, almost defiantly. I ignored him and went in the flat, but I opened the curtains and he still sat there staring at me. Finally he jumped straight up to the roof, a ten-foot jump, and ran up on top of the house; I could hear him scrabbling around up there for awhile.

"Do you know, for the next two or three weeks I would find him sitting in the street by my parking place when I came home from work. He'd be there staring at me three or four times a week. Of course I don't want strange cats around the garden, so I would try to chase him away. In a way it was funny; he'd run a few feet, then turn and stare at me, then run a few more feet again. He would dance a few feet ahead of me, almost as if he was taunting me. It was always the same, he would taunt me into following him into the garden, then he would run up the stairs, jump onto the railing, and then leap up to the roof and out of sight. And as I said, that is a ten-foot jump from the porch railing to the roof.

"Then the second set of unusual incidents began. This concerned my living room lights. I should explain that the room with the glass doors which I used as a dining room was originally intended as the living room. What had been a bedroom I now use as my living room—this room that we're in now. The affair of the lights began about a month after I'd moved here and after that cat started appearing. I came home and discovered the living room lights turned on. Of course, I thought I'd forgotten to turn the lights out when I left for work that morning. When it happened a second time I became annoyed with myself for being so forgetful. I realized, though, that I could have left them turned on and not noticed the lights during the day, because of my eye problems. So the next morning I made sure by double checking the light switch before leaving for work. I looked and also felt it to be certain the switch was down and read 'off.' But when I came home there was the switch up and the living room lights on again. Now, I was a little worried, since I was sure that the lights were off when I left in the morning. The only explanation I could find was that there had been a prowler or burglar during the day. But nothing was missing and, as far as I could tell, nothing was out of order in the house.

"The situation with the lights went on for several weeks, but I could see no evidence of a prowler in my flat and I missed nothing. Every morning I double-checked the light switch and was completely satisfied that it was off. But every night I'd find the lights turned on. Then once I came home at noon instead of at night to test the affair. Well, there they were, burning brightly again. I asked in the neighborhood, but nobody had seen any person around the house. Remember that the house had been completely rewired before I bought it; the wiring was new. At this point I had the switch inspected and was told that it wasn't faulty in any way. There was no reason for the lights turning on that I could see. And nobody had broken in. The glass doors are locked and latched from the inside, and the wooden door has a deadbolt lock. Friends looked and could find no sign of the locks being tampered with.

"Then, while I was still wondering what—or who— was causing the situation with the lights, the third event in this strange series began happening. You can see that on the sliding glass doors there is a handle on the outside, but no lock. The lock and latch is on the inside only, and

I always make sure that the doors are locked and latched at night. Yet one morning, when I was ready to leave, I found the doors unlatched from the inside. Again I put this down to my own forgetfulness. But when this happened a second time, I became alarmed, to say the least. There had been no prowlers, though, and I couldn't find signs of tampering with the locks. Well, I wondered if I was a sleepwalker. So one night, after I'd been ironing, I locked the doors and left the ironing board up when I went to bed. The board was up, across the doorway between my bedroom and the dining room, all night. And again in the morning the doors were unlatched. Now this couldn't have been sleepwalking; I would have fallen over the board, since there was no possible way around it. And this situation continued for some time, unlocked doors morning after morning.

"While all this was going on, I began to notice the smell of that cat—you know, cat spray—in the hallway right by my bedroom door. There is no way the cat could have come into the flat, since the only windows I leave open are on the street side and are second-story windows. And there are no vents or ventilation ducts from that spot to the roof. I simply couldn't account for this smell, which came time after time, even though I scrubbed the hall floor and walls.

"During this period when I smelled the cat, I had a peculiar thing happen several times when I was in bed. I felt something pressing on my legs at night when I was lying in bed. It was not a weight pressing on me—I don't know how to describe the sensation—neither a weight nor a pressure, but something that was there with me. First I assumed that it was the pressure of the blankets, but when it happened again, I became definitely curious. I wasn't afraid, but with all the other incidents building up, I was certainly becoming nervous.

"The final straw was the refrigerator defrosting for no reason at all. Mine is the frost-free type that I only turn to defrost once every six months, but at no other times. You can see the defrost dial here on the inside left wall; it is always left at the proper temperature. But one morning I opened the refrigerator door and discovered that it had completely defrosted. I looked and discovered the dial turned to the defrost position, but the door was closed tight before I opened it. And you can see that the dial is flush with the inside wall, so a person can't accidentally brush the dial with an arm when reaching in. And I am definitely not a sleepwalker—my sisters can verify that fact.

"With this defrosting experience I was definitely alarmed—yes, you could say that I was frightened. Not just by the refrigerator defrosting, or by the lights, or the other incidents. What frightened me was the way these things happened simultaneously, one occurrence after another until they were all going on at the same time. They built up in a series, one added to another. This is why I became frightened, the way these unnatural incidents piled one on top of another until I felt the situation was reaching a crisis. I realized that this whole affair was getting completely out of control and felt that it was better if I myself brought the affair to its climax. I had no choice at this point but to go to the priest at my parish.

"No, I don't think that I am easily disturbed or frightened, and I wouldn't consider myself superstitious or particularly suggestible. I did my best to account for this extraordinary behavior around my house on natural grounds, but I couldn't. Because of this I felt that I should explain matters to Father W——, put the affair into his hands, and ask for a formal exorcism.

"Before I went to the priest I wondered what his response would be. After all, he's known me and my family for years, so I was afraid that he might think I was going crazy. He listened to my whole story, though, and took the whole matter very seriously. I suppose he talked the affair over with the pastor and the church authorities—I don't know what the procedure is in such cases—and then he talked to me again. He said that, in his opinion, there was not sufficient cause to justify a formal exorcism, since there could still be rational explanations. He said, though, that considering the unusual character of the events and especially my reactions to them, he felt justified in coming to the house and giving a blessing. By this I mean that he came up and sprinkled the rooms and the hallway while he recited the prayers of the blessing. Then he blessed and sprinkled me with the holy water. And since that day of his blessing I haven't been bothered anymore. Except by that cat; I don't see him anymore, but occasionally I can smell him, so I think he is still around."

Miss McCarthy's responses to questions during the conversations of the affair are revealing in the way they indicate the attitudes of a pragmatic modern career woman toward the unexpected and the paranormal. Her first reaction to the odd incidents, she said, was simple curiosity, followed by annoyance at herself for what she felt was her own forgetfulness. Then, after searching for the natural explanations and finding none, she became alarmed and nervous. A prowler or burglar she could understand, but an unseen visitor, if such was the case, she could not. She was totally unprepared for supernormal phenomena, and unwilling to admit to herself that these could exist. She did not consider herself fanciful or superstitious and did not believe in ghosts or apparitions. As a Catholic she said that she accepted the existence of spirits, but did not believe that they linger in a house after death. As for the appearance of ghosts, she felt that such ideas were part of children's beliefs in ghost stories, haunted houses, and Halloween. Even as a child she had no interest in them, since her mother disapproved of these ideas as being superstitious and opposed to their traditional religious teachings. She stated that she found no practical explanation for the strange events, but she still seemed unwilling to admit that there could have been any supernormal cause. "Oh, I know that there must be some rational cause for all of this, but I can't find it," she said. "I'm almost forced to accept a spirit as the cause, since there have been no further incidents since my house was blessed. Maybe it was the cat, if that's possible. I know it sounds ridiculous, but that's what I think. The whole affair began with his weird appearances, and kept getting worse for almost three months."

Miss McCarthy told nobody of her experience except her priest, apart from asking friends to check her locks and doors for prowlers. She did not mention the matter to Mr. Chisholm when it happened, nor did she know of his experiences a year later when he was having them. This, she feels, discounts any possibility of suggestibility between close friends as being the explanations.

In conversation later, Mr. Chisholm confirmed Claire McCarthy's statement that neither knew of the other's experiences. He talked of the unusual incidents at his

149

apartment, which is about two miles west of Telegraph Hill in the Pacific Heights section of San Francisco.

The area in which Mr. Chisholm lives is one of tall, brick apartment buildings, most of which are twenty-five to thirty years old. His apartment is on the second floor of the building and consists of a living room, bedroom, dining alcove, kitchen, and bath. The living room and bedroom overlook the street. The entrance to his apartment is into a small foyer; to the right is the dining alcove and kitchen, while to the left are two adjacent doors leading to the living room and bedroom. The bathroom door opens from the foyer directly opposite the front entrance.

Mr. Chisholm uses the first room on the left as his bedroom and home office. The room had been intended by the builder as the apartment's living room, and the earlier tenants had followed this practice. Since the room is the largest in the apartment and has a large walk-in closet, Mr. Chisholm uses it as a combined bedroom and home office.

Born and brought up in New York City, Stuart Chisholm has lived in San Francisco for twelve years. At forty, he is an accounting graduate of Fordham University, and his manner shows the down-to-earth practicality of a CPA. He is of Scottish and Irish descent, and his sense of humor and witty manner of speech indicate his family background, while his approach to life follows the best traditions of American pragmatism. So, when confronted with the unexpected, he responded with complete realism in searching for an explanation on a rational basis; when none could be found, he accepted the situation cheerfully and realistically.

This is Mr. Chisholm's story:

"I moved to this apartment about two years ago after seeing it advertized for lease. It was large enough for all my things and on a quiet street, and I thought it would suit me well. I do quite a bit of tax work at home after work, so a quiet place is necessary for me. I hadn't known anyone who lived in the building before and didn't know anything about the former tenants of this apartment, but the place is well kept and soldily built with good, heavy doors and sound locks, so I took it. Well, about eighteen months ago after I'd been here some time, I began to notice that the front door of the apartment would be unlocked in the mornings when I was leaving for the office. As I've shown you, this door is double-locked by key. Naturally I thought that I'd forgotten to lock the door before going to bed. There is a nightlatch chain, but I don't use it since the door is double-locked from the inside. I started to check myself twice every night before going to bed to make sure that I'd locked the door. But even though I did, several times in the morning I'd find the front door unlocked, as if somebody had come in during the night. I would say that this happened about two dozen times over the past eighteen months. The door was never open, though, just unlocked.

"Then I began to notice something about this front door being unlocked. It always happened on those nights when I didn't completely close the door to the bedroom closet. That closet, you know, is a large walk-in type, about ten by four feet, and sometimes I don't completely latch the door, but just push it partly closed. Well, to make a long story short, I found that whenever I left this closet door in my bedroom open at night I would find the front door unlocked in the morning. And the reverse was true—I checked this carefully. It followed a definite pattern—only when I left my closet door open at night did I find the front apartment door unlocked in the morning. As if somebody—or something—was trying to come in at night.

"Then a few months after this door-unlocking began, I came home from work and discovered lipstick on the drinking glass in the bathroom. Now, my cleaning woman doesn't wear lipstick, so I assumed that some woman had been in the apartment during the day, possibly a woman who had a key to the apartment. I asked the apartment manager and found that only he had a key to the apartment, none of the earlier tenants, and that neither he nor his wife had been in the place. His wife works during the day and is not here at all. When I found the lipstick smears again I went to the house manager and asked if any other tenants in the building could have a key. He said no, and that the only woman home during the day was an old woman on the fifth floor who didn't wear lipstick.

"I've come home after work and found the lipstick on the glass about a dozen times I think; the last time was about two weeks ago. I looked around to see if anything was missing or out of place, or if there were any signs of someone coming in here. There weren't any. Nothing was stolen or misplaced, and I didn't even see footprints on the carpet; they're thick and would show impressions of a person walking around. But nothing.

"Well, after these strange things had been going on for a few months, about ten probably, I began to notice that there was someone in the room with me. No, I didn't see anything or hear any sounds. Let me put it this

152

way—at first I felt or sensed that I wasn't alone in the room. Then, on the later occasions, the feeling grew stronger and more positive that there was some person in the room with me. This happened only in the bedroom when I was working or reading or watching TV; I have my desk and TV in here. This feeling always came early in the evening, between eight and ten o'clock, and always when the closet door was open. Then I sometimes checked and found that the front door was unlocked again, even though I had locked it. It wasn't an unpleasant sensation, only strange, and very strong; I'd be reading or working and suddenly I would know that I wasn't alone, that there was another person in the bedroom, looking on and watching me. Several times I looked up from my work to see who was there, but there was nothing.

"This feeling of being watched only happened when the closet door was open, about a dozen times all told. Four or five times I woke up late at night and felt this person to be in the room with me, too, but this I put down to my being a light sleeper. There were no drafts, since this is a solidly built house with heavy, tight-fitting doors. I felt nothing except mentally that somebody was close beside me in the room.

"My first reactions were that either something was wrong with the doors or that somebody had a second key to the front door. But nobody has another key I'm told, and there has been no sign of a prowler by day. I made sure that the front door and lock were sound, and started using the nightlatch chain, though the unlocking still goes on. Apart from this and double-checking the lock at night, I haven't done anything.

"Since I knew that no person had been here that could be seen, I began to wonder who my visitor was that came at night and left the lipstick during the day. I suppose you could say that my attitude was simple curiosity. I just wanted to know who this woman was who came to visit me. Now, I've never really thought about ghosts or the supernatural at all. I suppose that I believe in the existence of spirits, but frankly I have never considered the subject as being of any importance.

"But, since I can't account for these incidents in any other way, I have to decide that the explanation might be supernatural or something. I don't want to believe this, but I can't give any other reason for this affair. And by the way, I'm anything but superstitious or suggestible. But if this affair isn't caused by a spirit, I don't know what could be causing it.

"By now I've gotten used to these peculiar visits— they're still going on, you see. But I'm not bothered at all by my visitor. Somehow I feel that if my visitor is a spirit, it is a woman who is friendly to me. I can't say why I feel this way, but whenever I sense that I'm not alone in the room I know somehow that my visitor is a woman. Actually, I feel comfortable when she is here. No, I'm not bothered; this is a big apartment, after all. If she wants to stay, there's room for two of us."

Like Miss McCarthy, Stuart Chisholm denied any previous interest in the supernatural or in Spiritualism, claiming that he knew nothing of psychical research or that serious studies had been done in this field. He had not, he said, ever read of such research in the supernormal, nor did he feel impelled to do so now even while undergoing experiences for which he could find no natural explanations. He felt that his profession and business interests more than filled his available time, and he showed no particular curiosity about the phenomena centering about his apartment or himself. If the unexplained happenings were caused by a ghost—and like Claire McCarthy, he seemed reluctant to admit as much—he said that he felt comfortable with his visitor and saw no reason to pursue the matter.

This, then, is how two realistic, haunted moderns tell of their reactions to the unexpected and of their different approaches to the unknown. Both people are university-trained and successful in their careers, happy and well-adjusted in their lives, having a wide circle of friends and a full range of intellectual interests and leisure activities.

They are, in fact, like you. Except that they have met and faced the unknown.

CHAPTER TWELVE

The Ghost in Fact

Of all the ghosts summoned here and brought back to the world of the living, two questions present themselves: Were these ghosts real in fact? Do they possess any common characteristics of behavior or conduct in their appearances?

In general these ghosts appeared as objective apparitions to their percipients, all of whom considered them to be real. The emotions inspired by the visits of the specters, however, have as little in common as the ghosts themselves. Some caused horror to those who saw or heard them, as with the presence that forced the lady to cover the mirror in the tower room of the Scottish castle. The Epworth poltergeist was less terrifying than enraging to the family, and the purposeless appearances of the phantom widow to the Morton family aroused curiosity more than anything else.

The only conclusion to be drawn from the behavior of the ghosts here is that, far from sharing any similar characteristics in their hauntings, they seem to appear at random, conforming to no discernible rules or patterns at all. While the poltergeist, for example, generally plagues a household with its infantile pranks, it is seldom heard to speak. Yet the Bell witch, some of whose performances were like the traditional poltergeist manifestations, also spoke, sang, and threatened the family and was, in some respects, almost as garrulous as Gef, the talking mongoose of the Isle of Man. The Morton ghost was seen as a solid and opaque figure and her footsteps could be heard in the corridors of the house, yet the lady who visited the San Francisco accountant made her presence known only by unlocking the apartment door and by leaving traces of her lipstick on a drinking glass. Some of the ghosts were seen and heard by several witnesses, others came only as solitary apparitions.

The Society for Psychical Research, which has been studying supernormal phenomena since 1882, seems to give a greater degree of credibility to apparitions occurring to more than one percipient. Too often the solitary phantom appearing only to one person must be discounted as being purely imaginative in origin. Even in the case of the ghosts of Versailles, the S.P.R. reviewer felt that, although two witnesses gave independent accounts of their experience, the basis for claiming the supernormal was entirely too slight, and gave too much indication of the weaknesses of human memory.

What are the tests for the reality of ghosts? To the psychical researcher, the objectivity of the apparition is foremost since the human mind and the five senses are all too fallible and liable to error. The immediacy of the report is also important, since it precludes errors in memory as well as permitting a disinterested investigation to be made of the phenomena, ideally while they are still occurring. If the ghost appears to more than one person and moreover is a spirit which manifests itself to a stranger or to a complete skeptic, the case is considerably strengthened. Then if investigation of the situation can be made while the phenomena are still occurring, as often happens with alleged poltergeist manifestations, steps can be taken to examine and sift the evidence and eliminate all fraudulent or purely imaginative elements. The remaining residue may then provide some evidence, however slight, to prove the case in favor of the reality of the ghost.

Consider the Morton ghost. Here the spectral widow appeared to at least seven observers, many of whom were practical and scientifically inclined adults. Attempts were made to prove the tangibility and solidity of the mysterious figure through photography, string experiments, and attempts at communication. None were successful, although the manner in which the ghostly widow passed through the strings fastened across the staircase indicated that the figure was not human, even though she appeared as a living person.

The poltergeist which annoyed the Wesley family was reported by several members of the family, with the exception of Hetty who seemed to be bothered most by the spirit of Old Jeffery. Here is the chief objection to the story by most students of the affair; the one person not telling of the manifestations of the so-called spirit may well have been the person who caused them.

With the Fox sisters, this was certainly the case. The rapping of the messages of the spirit was admittedly caused by the young girls in an effort to amaze and frighten their mother. But it is not clear how much the girls knew of the story of the murdered peddler, supposedly buried in the Hydesville cellar. Did they hear the story from their elders before they began their deliberate hoax, or did they gather the details and information during the nightly gatherings in the farm house, possibly through extrasensory perception?

The manifestations of the Bell witch and her deliberate hatred toward John Bell can be safely assumed to result from the disturbed personality of his daughter, Betsy. But here, too, while the case is of great interest to the modern psychiatrist, the parapsychologist and psychical researcher can find much to study. How were the phenomena accomplished by that unconscious portion of Betsy Bell's personality, and through what means, psychical or otherwise, was her father's personality and health so profoundly manipulated and affected?

In the accounts given by the two close friends in San Francisco of their experiences in their apartments, it is unfortunate that they did not compare the situations while they occurred. This attitude is completely typical of the modern skeptic in such matters, naturally; they don't want to accept the evidence of their senses. But considering the similarity of the occurrences and the close mental bonds between the friends, the events might have proved fruitful for psychical researchers in investigating the possibilities of the existence of telepathy and extrasensory perception.

If there are conclusions to be drawn then about stories of hauntings and of real ghosts, it might be that it is too soon to give any final opinion. The study of psychical phenomena, parapsychology, is in its infancy; the phenomena themselves are too random and varied in their nature. And what of ghosts? Where they were once the province of the theologian, then of the storyteller, and now of the ghost hunter, perhaps in the future science may give us the explanation through psychical research. Of this we are sure; the ghost has survived many explanations, and many onslaughts by the skeptic, and by this has proven the existence of the almost limitless capacity and variety of the mind of man and of his spirit.